Praise for
Sit in the Frequency of Change

"This is the book our turbulent times have been waiting for. Drawing from her unique integration of scientific rigor and spiritual wisdom, Dr. Claudia Thompson's Sit in the Frequency of Change *illuminates a revolutionary path to personal transformation. Through her four-step approach, she bridges logic and intuition, offering practical tools to break free from limiting patterns while accessing authentic wisdom. Having walked this path herself, Dr. Claudia Thompson guides others through their journey of faith and healing, showing how to transmute life's changes into opportunities for profound growth. This compassionate guide reveals how we can align with change's natural rhythms, tap into our innate resilience, and discover that love serves as our most potent resource for transformation."*

— Dr. Brandon Nappi, Executive Director of Leadership Programs at Yale's School of Divinity

SIT IN THE FREQUENCY OF CHANGE

Hay House Titles of Related Interest

YOU CAN HEAL YOUR LIFE, the movie,
starring Louise Hay & Friends
(available as an online streaming video)
www.hayhouse.com/louise-movie

THE SHIFT, the movie,
starring Dr. Wayne W. Dyer
(available as an online streaming video)
www.hayhouse.com/the-shift-movie

***

THE ANATOMY OF AWAKENING: The 5 Hidden Codes to Activate Self-Healing, Unlock Your Higher Consciousness, and Live Your Divine Destiny, by Dr. Sue Morter

THE AWAKENED WAY: Making the Shift to a Divinely Guided Life, by Suzanne Giesemann

DEAR CYCLE BREAKER: Wisdom and Practical Magic for Reclaiming the Wild Divine Feminine, by Dusah Wiseman

FORGIVE EVERYONE FOR EVERYTHING: 21 Days to Clear Your Mind, Heal Your Heart, and Manifest a Meaningful Life, by Iyanla Vanzant

SIT IN THE FREQUENCY OF CHANGE

A Four-Step Path to Embracing Life's Transformations and Unlocking Your Authentic Self

DR. CLAUDIA THOMPSON

HAY HOUSE LLC
Carlsbad, California • New York City
London • Sydney • New Delhi

Published in the United States by: Hay House LLC, www.hayhouse.com®
P.O. Box 5100, Carlsbad, CA, 92018-5100

Cover design: Terri Sirma
Interior design: Julie Davison
Image on page 109: Courtesy of the author

Cataloging-in-Publication Data is on file at the Library of Congress.

Tradepaper ISBN: 978-1-4019-9846-2
E-book ISBN: 978-1-4019-9847-9
Audiobook ISBN: 978-1-4019-9848-6

1st Printing

Printed in the United States of America

This product uses responsibly sourced papers, including recycled materials and materials from other controlled sources.

The authorized representative in the EU for product safety and compliance is Penguin Random House Ireland, Morrison Chambers, 32 Nassau Street, Dublin D02 YH68, Ireland. https://eu-contact.penguin.ie

Remember, Beautiful,

falling from Grace is a chance to rise.

This book is dedicated to
all the versions of me,
and all the versions of you,
who have learned and will learn to
sit in the frequency of change.
To the ones past, and the
ones I have yet to meet,
I love you.
You've got this.
Keep going.

CONTENTS

INTRODUCTION

If you're holding this book, there's a part of you that already knows something in your life is shifting and changing. You can feel it deep down, in the space you know is there but you're not really sure what it is yet, the space where your soul whispers and you feel the invisible nudge of fate. And no, it's not an accident you picked up this book. Everyone I've ever helped and guided has been led right to me—allowing us to cross paths through the force of divine timing and synchronicity.

This book found you because you're ready to move through change in a whole new way.

In this way, you stop trying to force an outcome, and you stop trying to "fix" yourself. This book will teach you how to sit in the change you need. Feel the vibration of its power, while learning to trust, as the world you once lived in rearranges around you.

What you'll find here is the path to start walking yourself home to the truest, most connected, and authentic version of you there is—a permission slip to drop the pressure of "doing it right" and simply remember and live as who you really are.

Sit in the Frequency of Change is part guidebook, part energetic transmission. It's the road map I wish I had when my own awakening cracked me wide open. It has the knowledge I was grasping for but carrying the entire time. In this book you'll find the aha activations of awakening, with the guideposts and lanterns illuminating your way through the depths of your soul.

I walked this path alone and in the dark, not because I was being punished by some judgmental God, but because I carry the codes of the liminal space, the in-between of what was and what is yet to be. And it's my job to share them with you. And to remind you, that no matter how lonely this path may feel at times, you're deeply supported and you'll find your way.

Held within these pages you'll find a mix of neuroscience, nervous system wisdom, spiritual insight, mystical truths, and energetic guidance—all grounded in the messiness of being human.

This book was written to meet you where you are. Because whether you're in the midst of a chaotic transition or a deep healing season or are finally ready to live the way your soul has been whispering (and sometimes shouting) about for years, you're exactly where you're meant to be. This is a blueprint to walk yourself home—a teacher, a mirror, a reminder that what you're going through and how you feel does not make you crazy—and most importantly, a reminder that you are not alone.

This book is divided into four main sections, with each section being a pillar of awakening. There's no one right way to move through these sections and chapters—just like there's no one right way to move through an awakening of who you are.

You can move through it front to back or trust your intuition to guide you to the chapter or section that calls to you right now. The Contents is intentionally detailed to allow you to move through the book as you wish—so you're easily able to reference and return to the chapters and sections that need your attention. There may be chapters you let marinate for weeks and sections that you cry through, reread, and pull forth massive amounts of clarity. Others may be a simple confirmation of what you already know to be true. Let each chapter, each section, be what it is for you in the moment you experience it.

Throughout the book you will find real-life, practical solutions for implementing and embracing your authenticity. I would encourage you to use every tool, every practice available in these pages, at least once. Allow yourself to discover your practice and what works for you—and the only way to do that is to take messy action figuring out what feels in alignment with you.

There's no need to rush your healing.

This isn't a read-once-and-shelve-it kind of book. It's designed to be revisited, reflected on, and integrated over time. Remembering who you are happens in layers—layers you cannot force or schedule. Integration of your authentic energy can take years. So let your energy decide the pace. Take the time you need to process—what's been hiding will be illuminated. You will get to where you'd like to be. Honor the timing and pace of your journey.

This book will ask you to be honest about your patterns, your fears, and your conditioning. You'll be invited to look at all the things you may have been consciously or unconsciously avoiding. Because the truth is, we can only ever fully come home to ourselves by witnessing all of who we are.

I will ask you to believe—even just a little bit—
that the version of you on the other side of this
transformation is already inside you.
Waiting. Ready. Whole.

This process isn't about becoming someone new. It's about remembering who you've always been. There may be chapters that feel raw, like you've been ripped open. Others will feel like a deep exhale. Expect resistance, grief, anger, love, and joy to be present. All of it is welcome here. Your only job is to stay present and show up for yourself.

Let the energy move.

I didn't write this book from some pedestal of an all-knowing enlightenment. I wrote it from inside the messy, beautiful, painful, powerful process of awakening and rebuilding who I am. I've been where you are—not knowing what's coming next, unsure of who I am without the thought patterns and behaviors I ran on repeat. I'm still healing and learning to trust my own energy, reminding myself to stay when things get uncomfortable. What I've downloaded, remembered, integrated—and will continue to practice and embody day in and day out—is what I'm sharing with you here.

My promise is that I'll be honest with you. I won't sugarcoat the work that has to be done, but I will always remind you of your power. I'll hold the highest frequency for your transformation, even if you forget it for a while because *I can see* the timelines we have the ability to anchor.

I'll remind you that your soul chose this life for a reason. And that the agreements you made with Source were never about performing some watered-down version of yourself for the world—they were about you anchoring in a full remembrance and embodiment of all that you are.

You already have everything you need inside you.

This book is here to help you hear it, see it, feel it more clearly.

Come as you are. Bring your fear, your curiosity, your exhaustion, your courage. This is your official invitation from Source, your guides, your higher self, your soul, to slow down, tune in, and *sit in the frequency of change.*

I know you're ready . . . or you wouldn't be here.

You've got this. Keep going.

PART I

Rise

This part of the journey begins at the edge—where the life we've known starts to dissolve, and something deep down calls us forward. Rise isn't about quick fixes, spiritual bypassing, or fluff. It's about waking up—opening your eyes—and hearing the call from deep within you that says, "Something more is meant for me. I just don't know how to reach whatever it is yet."

We don't rise by bypassing what hurts. We rise by choosing to meet it—with eyes wide open, an unguarded heart, and the courage to begin again.

In this section, you will reconnect with simple truths that were never really lost—only buried under the noise of conditioning, chaos, and survival. Every one of us comes into this world buried under something, and these truths exist to help you remember who you are and why you're here.

We explore Faith—not the kind taught through mechanisms of control and fear, but the kind that introduces you to the energy that whispers, "You've got this. Keep going" when the world goes silent. You'll meet the Faith that stands beside you when you feel you've walked into the fires of an awakening . . . and you'll learn to hold her hand as you continue to take the steps on your path.

This is a path that will always include the Dark Forest—the space no one volunteers to walk through, yet we all find ourselves there. Through this initiation you'll face what's been avoided. You'll meet the shadows and strip away every part of you that isn't really you at all.

From this space you will learn to find your center, the space where you find peace in the chaos of the world and you begin to remember who you are and why you're here.

Rise is the beginning of coming home to yourself.

It's where we get honest about who we are . . . and who we are not. It's where we feel the full weight of what was and where we choose to believe in what could be. If you're reading this, you're already digging yourself out from what you've been buried under—you found your way here, and I'm so happy you did.

This is the awakening of your highest, most authentic self.

Move through these chapters at your soul's pace and return to them as often as you need. *Rise* is the grittiest part of the journey. It's where you access your energy at a depth and understanding you've never touched before.

Honor the space and time that's required.

You've got this. Keep going.

CHAPTER 1

SIMPLE TRUTHS

Life is a series of unseen agreements—bargains we made between us and our Creator. These agreements aren't written down or handed to us at birth, yet they shape every aspect of our lived experience. They are the unspoken truths governing the very essence of being human. The invisible threads weaving through the fabric of the human experience—influencing our choices, our challenges, and even our potential for growth. *Simple truths are the bargains we made for our lived experience.*

Understanding the bargains governing the soul's experience in this realm gives us access to the framework of life itself. Source left us guides for our journey, and we just need to learn where to look. Simple truths aren't meant to limit us, but they are the boundaries of this realm—when we understand and accept them for what they are, we open ourselves up to a life filled with deeper meaning, purpose, and a lot more ease.

The simple truths of this world are the foundation our entire journey exists within. They shape our experiences, define our challenges, and hold the key to our most profound transformations. Accepting these bargains as simple truths of our experience lowers the level of resistance as we move through life. Challenges that once felt insurmountable become easy to navigate.

Simple truths help us understand the bargains we made for life, and they give us access to the perspective we need to begin to see how we are an important part of a much bigger story. The obstacles we face, the setbacks, and the things we once perceived as failures are all opportunities to turn something difficult into something beautiful.

Life is not a series of random events. Your life is filled with beautiful, meaningful opportunities for transformation.

Life's challenges become a lot more bearable when we understand they are part of the larger bargain we made with Source. When we look at all the hard things we've experienced and see them as an invitation to deepen our connection with our true self instead of as something to be endured, we elevate our experience. *The moments that bring us to our knees force us to rise.* You signed up for this experience because of the challenge, not in spite of it. Reaching your highest potential is something you were built to do, and when you integrate the simple truths of life, you gain the tools you need to elevate faster and easier.

As you move through this chapter, you'll learn to see these simple truths as the foundation of the lived experience here—a way to interpret the twists and turns of your journey with greater clarity and purpose. Each truth you integrate acts as a lens, helping you to see your life's purpose in better focus, even when the world around you feels uncertain or uncomfortable at times.

Integrating life's simple truths is not about avoiding life's difficulties; it's about transforming your relationship with them. It's about seeing that your agreements with Source are not here to break you down but to break you open—helping you reach the parts of yourself you didn't realize you had access to.

By embracing this understanding, you empower yourself to navigate life from your true north, accessing your highest and most authentic self with trust, Faith, and a renewed commitment to growth.

As we go deeper into these simple truths, you'll begin to understand that life's greatest challenges are not random—they're a tailored set of circumstances designed to wake you up to your own potential. And while I know firsthand how hard life can be (cue abandonment, abuse, disordered eating, divorce, and a rock bottom self-worth), understanding the bargains we made for life in this realm gives us the framework we need to realize life is not happening to us, it's happening for us.

IT'S JUST LIKE THIS FOR NOW

Life is impermanent. From the moment we incarnate into our body, we enter a silent agreement with Source—everything we know and experience is in a constant state of flux. The simple truth of mortality is understanding that life is fleeting. We agree to loss, change, and ultimately death as an inherent part of being alive. But the impermanence of life isn't a flaw; it's a part of the experience here. It's woven into the fabric of everything inside and all around us. Death and rebirth is visible everywhere on Earth—mirrored through the cycles of nature, reflecting the rhythms of our lives.

Every transformation on Earth is a reminder that beginnings look an awful lot like endings. Our lives play out waves of experiences as we move through joy, sorrow, growth, death, and rebirth. Embracing the impermanence of life's lived experience is understanding these waves are not random occurrences but the natural ebb and flow of the human experience.

Accepting this simple truth gives us the opportunity to create peace in an ever-shifting world.

Life becomes a whole lot easier when we accept change as the only constant—that holding on too tightly to anything will result in suffering. We resist change when we fear the unknown—when we cling to what feels familiar even when it no longer serves us. The beauty of change is in the invitation to let go, to trust and surrender to the flow of life.

Surrendering to how consistent change is in life isn't about giving up or letting go of our dreams—it's an acknowledgment of the divine intelligence that sends manifestations in surprisingly beautiful ways. *We can know exactly what is meant for us without having any idea how we will get there.* There's an energy of divine ease when we release our illusion of control—when we settle into Source's ability to infinitely bless us if we simply allow the blessings to flow.

Learning to navigate the highs and lows of our lives isn't an easy task. We're faced with seemingly insurmountable loss at times—loss that comes with incredibly dense emotions to navigate. But if we can learn to navigate these moments with the understanding that change is a simple truth of this realm, we move through the density of our lived situations with Grace. We embody the knowing that it's just like this for now. Whether it feels dense, light, or some combination of both . . . it is just like this for now.

Nothing is permanent. We and the world are ever-changing. It's a simple truth.

I know firsthand what it's like to fight this truth . . . and I know what it's like to embrace it. *Fighting is far more difficult.* I spent decades of my life fighting—to find love in all the wrong places, repeating generations of trauma, and feeling stuck in the depths of the shadow experience that was my life. I've battled myself and my body. Waging war with disordered behaviors, fighting my ability to feel, and grasping for control. I've hoped to become numb—like so many of us do. I've stayed far too long in relationships that were completely out of alignment with who I was and who I am. I spent decades trying to fit in some box I never belonged in—*and I fixed it all by simply letting go.* By allowing everything to ebb and flow and change around me. I stopped holding on to everyone and everything. I embraced this simple truth:

The life I knew deep down I was destined for required a lot of change.

Embracing change is the key to drawing in the future you want. There is peace and joy to be found in the freedom of not having to figure it all out on your own—in allowing Source to work its magic in your life.

That's not to say you won't experience very real and painful loss. When we lose something we love—a person, a dream, a way of life—we're confronted with the reality that while things are working out for our highest good, it won't always pan out the way we had hoped it would. *Sometimes those we hold dear don't get to come with us, and sometimes we have to pivot hard to get to where we need to be.* There's powerful transformations lying in these difficult moments. Opportunities to strip away the illusions we hold on to—finding deeper truths our soul holds just below the surface.

Mine was my dear friend Sam—she saw me when I couldn't even see myself. We met at the depths. I was going through a painful and ugly divorce while she was battling a cancer that no one could figure out how to cure. Two souls plunged into the darkness found friendship where outside circumstances would've dictated otherwise. It was the promise I made to her after she passed a couple of months before her 30th birthday that broke me open in ways I had no idea were possible. *She led me down the very path that opened up my abilities.* She helped me gain access to other realms—by showing me who I really am.

The pain of loss cracks us open
in ways nothing else can.

It forces us into the depths of our emotions. It forces us to feel, and it forces us to ask bigger questions: Who are we? Where do we belong? How do we move forward? And what fills the void? Loss creates the vulnerability we need to wake us up to who we are—it's how awakenings start. Space is created so that we discover the parts of ourselves we didn't realize were there. That's where creation happens. That's how we manifest our most beautiful and aligned selves—moving through loss, through change.

When we're faced with the truth of our limited time here we're given a choice: We can explore the unknown, releasing attachments to everyone and everything along the way, or we can hold on to what's fleeting for dear life, missing our opportunity to truly experience the beauty of transformation through unconditional love here on Earth.

Endings make way for beautiful beginnings. There is a frequency to your soul that exists beyond this realm, and when you sit with Grace long enough, you finally start to see how beautiful your losses can be. How they help just as much as they hurt.

When we stop fighting for control of every last thing, we open ourselves up to a deeper experience. We gain access to the love, joy, and connection that exists just beyond what the eyes can see.

Every transformational moment is a part of a much bigger story—and if we let go, we're led right to the highest versions of ourselves.

PAIN IS INEVITABLE; SUFFERING IS OPTIONAL

Experiencing life on Earth comes with the bargain of experiencing pain. Incarnating here includes discomfort, heartbreak, disappointment, and grief as necessary parts of our journey. We aren't being punished. Pain is a teacher—guiding us toward growth and transformation. It breaks us open and it asks us to dismantle the illusions we cling to, expanding our awareness and access to who we truly are.

Pain has the uncanny ability of cutting through the noise—insisting that we confront the parts of ourselves we run from, hide, and deny. It forces us to pay attention to what really matters, and it asks us to face the deeper questions about our purpose, our choices, and the meaning of our lives. As much as we try to avoid it, pain finds a way in, acting as a catalyst for the evolution of our soul. Pain provides a powerful opportunity—to lean in and discover what lies on the other side of it.

The simple truth is that without pain, there is no growth. Our highest potential is accessed through the density of our experiences—it isn't handed to us. Each moment of pain contains a layer of our awakening. It's an invitation to transform, a call to shed the current layer of ourselves, making room for a higher alignment.

While pain is inevitable, suffering is a choice left up to us.

Understanding this truth makes life a whole lot easier. Pain comes from the experiences shaping us—loss, heartbreak, disappointment. Suffering, on the other hand, is the result of our resistance to the pain we experience. It's what happens when we refuse to accept the reality of our circumstances, when we cling to the belief that life should be different than it is.

Suffering thrives in the gaps between what we want and what currently is. It's birthed from our unwillingness to let go of control and our refusal to accept divine timing in our lives. We suffer not because we feel pain but because we fight it, deny it, and try to escape from it. We build walls around us to protect ourselves from hurt, not realizing that we trapped the pain, keeping it inside through our own bricks of resistance.

Understanding the difference between pain and suffering is the integration of this simple truth. *We have a choice in how we respond to the challenges of life.* Pain is unavoidable, and we can improve our experience with it when we drop the mental and emotional struggle against it. We can choose to accept the things we cannot change, or we can choose to perpetuate our own misery with stories that turn a moment of pain into a lifetime of anguish.

What if we leaned in to the pain? What if we allowed ourselves to fully feel—without trying to fix it or change it? What if we embodied everything it is to be human, including the pain? This is where the magic of alchemy is. In our ability to transform the painful into something beautiful. Leaning in to the discomfort of it all doesn't mean we have to like it or that we seek more of it. It simply means we accept this simple truth: that we experience pain without it being all-consuming.

When we stop fighting the reality of pain and surrender to its presence, we unlock the ability to heal.

Instead of seeing pain as a punishment or curse, we see it as a guiding force. We realize that the discomfort of life is not an enemy but a doorway to the deeper truth our soul longs to understand.

The human experience is messy—growth arrives through our most difficult moments. That means we have to trust, no matter how painful it is, that we have the strength within us to navigate whatever crosses our path. Because when we do, we begin to see that we are not our pain—we are the awareness that experiences it.

The greatest life transformations occur when we stop avoiding or attempting to eliminate pain. *When you approach pain with compassion and curiosity, you become the alchemist, removing resistance at every turn.* You learn to appreciate the beauty of painful transformations, and suffering loses its grip in that space between where you are and where you want to be.

Pain is a guide.

It shines light on the areas of your life that need attention, care, and change. It strips away the masks you wear, exposing the truth of who you are and what you truly value. Pain has the power to show you where you are out of alignment—the places where you aren't being true to yourself. And while the lessons of pain are not easy, they are necessary. Pain is a universal motivator. It forces action.

Every painful experience has the potential to quantum leap you through to the next layer of your awakening. It asks you to slow down, listen deeply, and reflect on what matters most—allowing you to find gratitude in the most dire of moments. Pain teaches you about resilience, compassion, and how unbreakable the spirit really is.

When we encounter pain, we learn how capable we really are.

When you embrace the lessons of pain, you start to see how your struggles are not a sign of weakness but an opportunity to create more courage and strength. Pain breaks you down so you can rise from the rubble—a guide leading you to your highest, most authentic self.

Obstacles are really opportunities for growth.

Alchemize the pain.

YOU ARE BOTH THE CREATOR AND THE CREATION

You enter life with the bargain of co-creation with your Creator. This simple truth shows you that you're an active participant, shaping your reality, while you are simultaneously an expression of a greater universal force—Source. Life is a dance between conscious creation and divine orchestration, between your will and the divine timing of life.

Life is not something that happens to you; it's something that unfolds through you. Every thought we think, every belief we hold, every action we take creates the life we experience. We are co-creators with the universe—holding immense power to shape our reality. The simple truth of co-creation is a profound recognition of personal responsibility. Our internal world projects itself onto our external reality—life on this planet reflects who we all are and what we are thinking and believing.

It's tempting to view the challenges we face as mere coincidences or external forces, but in reality, a lot of what we experience is a direct reflection of what our internal state looks like. The universe responds to the energy that we emit. When we accept this truth, we are empowered to take responsibility for our internal state of affairs—the parts of our lives that we wish to change. Limiting beliefs, fear, and doubt manifest into our external reality—so does love, abundance, and trust.

You can become the architect of your greatest transformations through radical responsibility.

Co-creation invites you to explore your beliefs and intentions with curiosity. Every limiting belief, every subconscious pattern, and every unexamined thought holds the potential to shape your reality. You're bargaining with the universe every day through your energy. It's a constant dialogue. *Are you speaking the language of love, abundance, and trust?* Or are you communicating fear, lack, and resistance?

The reality you experience isn't just happening—you experience what you're drawing to you through your beliefs, thoughts, and feelings.

Personal responsibility is the key to unlocking this truth. Our lives are the sum of the choices we make, and it's up to us to consciously respond to the things the universe presents. Every thought, belief, and decision is a brushstroke on the canvas of your life. Your thoughts create your feelings, your feelings drive your actions, and your actions shape your reality. If you want to experience something different, it starts with taking responsibility for how you view your own stories.

The beauty of this truth is that you are never stuck. As creators, we always have the power to shift into a different reality. If you don't like the chapter you are in, you can write a new one. But this requires self-awareness—the willingness to wake up and examine your beliefs, patterns, and actions with honesty and compassion. *You have to muster the courage to look in the mirror and not run from what you see.*

Personal responsibility doesn't mean that we are in control of every detail of our lives. We are an intricate part of the web of consciousness expressing itself—which means we will experience events we'd rather avoid. The key to this truth doesn't lie in controlling every event but in our response to what presents. That's where our power lies. Because while we are creators, we are also creations of a force that is the Source of everything.

Understanding this truth is to dance between the realms of control and surrender, flowing between the assertion of your will and trusting what unfolds.

It's this delicate balance where magic happens. Control and surrender are not opposing forces; they are complementary energies guiding your path. Control allows you to take inspired action, to set intentions, and to shape your reality with purpose. Surrender asks you to release attachment to outcomes, to trust that Source has a plan greater than what you, or anyone, can see.

Many of us struggle with the need for control. We want things to go a certain way, at a certain time, in a specific order. But the truth is, life rarely works out that way. There are going to be times where no matter how much you plan or try to control the outcome, things don't happen the way you wanted. This is where surrender comes in.

Surrendering doesn't mean you give up on your desires or passively accept whatever comes your way. Rather, it's about trusting the process—trusting Source is working in your favor, even when you can't see how. It's about letting go of the need to micromanage every aspect of your life and creating the space for the divine to intervene in ways that are more beautiful and aligned than you could ever imagine.

The balance of control and surrender is an art.

It requires intuitive discernment to know when to assert your will in the form of inspired action and when to step back and allow life to unfold, to have the ability to hold a vision for the future while being flexible enough to pivot when things don't go as planned.

The tension between control and surrender is fundamental to the human experience. Learning when to take the reins and when to release them requires a deep trust in yourself and in the larger forces at play. This tension between control and surrender is where true growth happens. You develop the wisdom to recognize that, as a creator, you are powerful, but as a creation, you are also part of a much larger, divine design. You learn to trust that even when you can't see how, you will get to where you are destined to go.

The power to create lies within your beliefs. What you believe about yourself, your life, and the world around you directly influences what you experience. If you hold beliefs rooted in lack, fear, or unworthiness, your reality will mirror those beliefs. You can shift your reality by changing to beliefs rooted in love, abundance, and possibility instead.

You can rewire the foundation of what you believe.

Manifestation is the process of aligning our beliefs, thoughts, and actions with the reality we want to create. It's about recognizing that we are constantly in conversation with the universe through our energy. When we believe in our power to create, when we trust in the possibility of what we desire, we become magnetic to the opportunities, people, and experiences that align with that belief.

The key to manifesting is alignment—ensuring your thoughts, beliefs, and actions are all in the same frequency band. It's not enough to simply wish for something. You must believe it's possible and take inspired action toward it.

This principle is the very reason you are reading this book. I held a vision of its publication, I took inspired action in the form of drafting without any clue how I would connect with a publisher, and I trusted in Source's ability to align me with the perfect people. I was contacted by this very publisher, asking if I would be interested in publishing a book with them while I was drafting this very book. I co-created this experience with Source.

What is truly meant for you will find you in the most unexpected of ways—if you simply believe, take inspired action, and then get out of Source's way, you will manifest your highest alignment.

Practical Steps for the Simple Truth of Co-Creation:

- **Identify limiting beliefs:** Take time to reflect on the beliefs you hold about yourself and your life. Notice any recurring patterns or narratives that don't align with your highest vision. Ask yourself: *What do I believe about my worth, my capabilities, and my potential?* Work on developing higher aligned beliefs.
- **Reframe your thoughts:** Challenge your limiting beliefs by consciously reframing them into empowering ones. For example, replace *I'm not good enough with I am worthy of all that I desire.* This practice shifts your energy and aligns your thoughts with the reality you want to create.
- **Visualize your desired reality:** Spend time each day visualizing the life you want to manifest. See yourself living it fully, feeling the emotions associated with your vision. Visualization strengthens the energetic connection between your current reality and your desired outcome.
- **Take inspired action:** Co-creation requires more than just intention; it requires action. Pay attention to the intuitive nudges and inspired ideas that arise. Trust yourself enough to follow through on them, even if they lead you into unfamiliar territory.
- **Release attachment to outcomes:** Surrender the *how* of your desires to the universe. Trust that divine timing is at play, and remain open to the unexpected ways your manifestations might unfold. Release the need to control every detail and allow the universe to work its magic.

Co-creation is not about forcing reality to conform to your will. It's about aligning with the flow of life while consciously choosing your direction. Recognize your power to shape your experience and embrace your role as a creator while honoring the magic of being a creation within a greater whole.

The simple truth that we are both creators and creations invites us to explore our relationship with Source. It asks you to step into your power without losing sight of the greater good. It calls you to take responsibility while surrendering to the forces that guide your path.

When we embrace this simple truth, we find harmony within and with the world around us.

Life is not happening to you, but through you, in a divine collaboration with Source.

We are all walking each other home.

LOVE IS THE ULTIMATE CURRENCY

Love is the currency of life. It can't be measured in dollars or possessions, and at the same time, it's the ultimate measure of our wealth. When we strip away all the external markers of success, the only thing that remains is the love we have given and received. Love transcends material boundaries and connects us with the essence of who we are at the soul level. Love is the force that gives life meaning—the very energy that fuels connection, joy, and fulfillment.

Love is the frequency of Source.

Everything we seek in life—whether it's abundance, belonging, or growth—comes back to the vibration of love as the central force. Without love, we are left with an emptiness that no amount of external success can fill.

At the heart of all love is self-love. It's the foundation upon which everything else sits. We cannot truly give and receive love if we do not love ourselves first. This simple truth is both transformative and challenging. Self-love is not about being self-centered or egotistical; it's about embracing the depths of who we are and authentically expressing ourselves. It's about recognizing our inherent worth and treating ourselves with the same compassion and understanding we offer to others.

When you learn to love yourself unconditionally, as Source intended, you align with the energy you need to genuinely give and receive love. *It's not a selfish act—it's an essential one.* It means setting boundaries to protect your well-being, prioritizing your needs, and treating yourself with kindness. Without self-love, you're left seeking validation from external sources, never fully able to accept or believe in the love you receive.

Self-love requires releasing the narratives keeping you from accepting yourself fully—the stories that weave the energy that you are not enough throughout your life. These beliefs, ideas, and experiences are not in alignment with your highest, most authentic self, the part of you that understands that you come from love, so you are love.

There isn't a single moment of your life where you are not worthy.

Learning to love yourself, in all your moments, is the foundation of your highest alignment. It requires that you accept and love your authenticity.

This truth is simple: Love—true unconditional love—is what's required for the life you want to live. *Love is the force that connects us all—transcending the boundaries of our world.* Learn to love yourself, and you'll completely transform your experience on this planet.

YOU ARE NOT SEPARATE FROM THE WHOLE

Life doesn't happen in isolation. We are all part of a beautiful, interconnected web of consciousness that binds everything together. The simple truth is, we are never truly alone. Every experience, every person, every encounter has an invisible thread connecting it all. We are all a part of all that is—which means our individual experiences are a part of a larger, collective existence.

Existing is understanding the bargain that we are all connected, pieces of the greater whole. Every action you take, every word you speak, and every thought you entertain ripples through the web of consciousness, impacting not just your life but everyone else's. *What we do to others, we do to ourselves, and vice versa.* This simple truth challenges us to see beyond the boundaries of our personal lives and expand our understanding of how we impact the world around us. Every interaction is an exchange of energy, weaving the threads that bind our stories together.

Interconnectedness is a foundational principle of our existence.

Science and spirituality blend seamlessly through this truth with quantum physics providing evidence of quantum entanglement—where particles remain connected, no matter the distance. In the same way, our souls are entangled with the universe and each other.

Despite our inherent connection, the human mind and ego can create an illusion of separation. They whisper narratives that reinforce a sense of isolation—making us feel that we are alone in our struggles. The illusion of disconnection leads to feelings of loneliness, division, and competition. We end up building walls between ourselves and others—walls we think are for protection but that ultimately end up isolating us.

The illusion of separation stems from the analytical brain's need to define and identify ourselves as distinct and different—a need arising from the fear centers of the brain. We often cling to the idea of a separate self to maintain another illusion: control. The deeper truth is we are one with all that is. The narrative that says "This is me, and that is you" is faulty from the very foundation.

Spiritual practices are designed to dissolve these illusions. Practicing meditation, breath work, and moments of stillness allow us to quiet the analytical brain's incessant chatter. In this space we can feel a deeper truth emerge—that beneath our stories and experiences, there is no separation.

We are all fractals of Source,
experiencing itself, through all of us.

When we accept this simple truth, we shift how we see the world, viewing it through a lens of connection and empathy. This truth allows us to notice that the judgments and separations we create are all illusions masking our deeply connected reality. Dissolving these illusions wakes you up from the dream—the world is not what you initially thought it was and you find it's more beautiful, more whole, and filled with more love than you realized.

One of the most tangible ways this interconnectedness reveals itself is through the signs and synchronicities we experience. These seemingly coincidental events are Source's way of communicating with us, guiding us, and affirming that we are on the right path. When you open yourself up to these experiences, you start to see that nothing in life is random—it's divinely orchestrated.

Synchronicity is a reminder that our lives are a part of a much larger blanket of existence, where every thread is interwoven with purpose.

You've likely experienced moments where the right person shows up at exactly the right time . . . moments where messages and opportunities found you when you truly needed them. These are not mere coincidences; they are signals from Source, helping you, guiding you, and affirming your connection to all that is.

As you move on the path toward aligning with your highest, most authentic self, Source will send signs to reassure and guide you. These can come in various forms—a meaningful number sequence that keeps appearing, an animal crossing your path, a song lyric that deeply resonates, or an unexpected encounter that changes your perspective. All these moments are a nod from Source, reminding you that you are supported, seen, and connected at all times.

By paying attention to these synchronicities, you can develop a deeper sense of trust in the plan for your life. They serve as a compass, navigating you to your highest alignment and reminding you that your journey doesn't exist in a vacuum—you are intertwined with the journey of others. When you need confirmation that you are not alone, synchronicity is there.

Our individual healing isn't just self-serving; it's a contribution to healing the collective. The more you heal yourself, the more you elevate the frequency of the whole. When you let go of shame, anger, and resentment, you don't just heal yourself—you create a movement of energy through the collective that touches the lives of everyone around you. Each person's healing impacts another's.

Healing is an act of love—
for ourselves and the world.

Every moment of compassion, every act of kindness, and every choice we make to see ourselves in others helps heal the world.

The simple truth that we are all connected is an invitation to manifest, not just for your highest good but for the highest good of all. You don't need to sacrifice your needs or lose your sense of self to do this. In fact, when you take responsibility for your energy and actions, you energetically encourage others to do the same.

Making aligned choices through love, being conscious of the energy we focus on and put into the world, and healing the parts of ourselves that seek to divide us moves us forward into elevated states of experience.

Express your authenticity while honoring others as they work to do the same.

We all elevate when we do.

When we understand the simple truths of this realm, we uncover a framework that guides us through the human experience with greater ease and clarity.

Life is no longer seen as a series of unrelated or random challenges, and integrating these truths into our daily lives drastically reduces the resistance we encounter.

Life's simple truths aren't abstract ideas; they're the bargains we've made for our lived experience. Each truth offers a path toward a more fulfilling life—a way to navigate your experiences and challenges while staying connected to your soul. When you embrace these truths, life doesn't necessarily become easier but the way in which you experience it does.

You find yourself feeling more supported and guided.

The magic of transformation happens when you embody these truths in your everyday life. Understanding them isn't enough; you must actively practice living in alignment with them. By doing so, you make conscious choices, acting from a place of love, connection, and trust in the unfolding of your journey.

Embracing these truths allows you to live more authentically—in alignment with your highest and most authentic self.

Align your decisions with who you truly are, not with who you think the world wants you to be. Living authentically means trusting these truths as a reliable compass, guiding you even in the most uncertain and uncomfortable moments. Every obstacle becomes an opportunity for growth and transformation. Each challenge becomes an invitation to practice what you know—so embody these simple truths in your thoughts, actions, and energy.

Living in alignment with these simple truths will not free you from hardship, but it will provide a sense of ease and clarity when navigating difficulties that have the ability to elevate your experience. You cannot avoid pain, but you can learn to approach it with purpose and peace. When we let go of the need to control every outcome, we find ourselves.

The freedom in these simple truths lies in your ability to release resistance and allow Source to reveal how good life can really get.

You've got this. Keep going.

CHAPTER 2

OUR RELATIONSHIP WITH FAITH

Faith is often misunderstood as a passive belief, a quiet request that something or someone will intervene on our behalf. But Faith is not passive. Faith is a powerful feminine force that guides us through fear. Faith is an active force—an energy that moves us forward in life, compelling us to trust in the unseen while taking bold steps into uncharted territory. This unwavering force is here to guide you and help you achieve the most fulfilling, purpose-filled life you can live. In order to accomplish this, you have to align with Faith.

To redefine Faith, we have to strip away all the passive thoughts and feelings associated with this energy. Faith is not about waiting for your external circumstances to change. And Faith is not blind optimism or wishful thinking either. Walking with Faith requires a conscious decision to trust in the process of life and to align with divine timing, even when your path is obscured with doubt, fear, and challenges seemingly everywhere. Faith is the energy that propels you forward when the logic of your analytical mind says to stop.

Faith is the voice that says, "You've got this. Keep going" just when you need it most.

I first started channeling the immensity of her energy as I took a massive trust fall in my own life. I was at a breaking point, standing in a small park next to the Brooklyn Bridge and debating whether I was going to upend my entire life and leave my then husband. It was my first trip to the city, and while I was in awe of the enormity, tired from the 20,000 plus steps I was taking every day, and loving the time away with my friends, the only thing I could pay attention to was the very loud voice in my head screaming that something had to change. And while I'm not going to go into great detail about my relationship, *because everything happens for a reason and people play the roles they're meant to play,* it wasn't good. The years leading up to this trip left me drained and almost completely detached from my energy. So, I had a moment in that park where I finally decided to listen to what I heard, and I started asking questions and making demands. *Okay, you want me to leave, then what?* Nothing. *Then show me. Before I get on the plane to go home, show me this can't be better. Show me I have to leave. "Okay."* I heard it plain as day. *Okay.* I don't know if I believed it in that moment, but my ex went down a path over the coming hours that I was not only familiar with but also was never going to escape unless I left. *She showed me before I got on the plane.* And on my way home, I held on to her for dear life as I unraveled my entire life in the coming weeks.

Faith is the energy that connects us with Source and our highest, most authentic self. She binds us to our highest purpose and reinforces the trust we need to fulfill that purpose. We are not being asked to place faith in something external but to sit with the energy of Faith so that we can feel deeply enough to believe in ourselves. Faith shows us that we have the ability to navigate life's challenges and opportunities, that we can grow and evolve and in divine timing manifest our highest reality. Faith empowers us to be something greater, to trust our instincts and intuition, to keep moving on our path and express our inner knowing of our true selves.

Your higher purpose is not some distant, elusive goal waiting to be found. It's woven into every moment and every interaction, a target drawing its arrow home. Faith is the bridge of energy linking you to this purpose. Aligning with Faith is an opportunity to hold the hand of the energy that sees your highest potential in every moment. In this world, we access Source by utilizing the bridge of energy Faith creates, and I pull her through every time I share a channeled message.

You've got this. Keep going.

Faith has the ability to anchor you—grounding your trust in a bigger picture that you cannot always see. Faith invites you to believe in the synchronicity of events, the wisdom of divine timing, and the beauty of life's unfolding. When you embrace Faith as a guiding force, you release control over every outcome, surrendering to the alignment that is playing out for the highest good. Your perspective shifts—seeing setbacks as redirections, doubts as opportunities to increase your trust, and challenges as catalysts for growth.

Faith is not passive; she's relentless.

Faith is the force that asks you to step forward when fear tells you to retreat. Her energy asks you to believe when doubt and uncertainty are everywhere. Faith is a living energy that supports you on your journey, and she sees how capable you really are.

The purpose of Faith is not to shield you from the hardships of life but to help you navigate them with courage and purpose. Faith asks that you trust in the unfolding of life, believing that no matter what is happening, each experience is part of a larger plan designed to help you grow and evolve. Faith teaches you to trust not only in Source's ability to support you but also in your own ability to rise to the challenges you face. You need Faith to see how capable you are—of so many beautiful things.

In this chapter, we're going to explore Faith, not as an abstract idea but as an essential energy that guides and empowers us. With Faith as our guide, we find our strength, gain clarity when we trust ourselves, and muster the courage to walk our paths, no matter how many twists and turns there may be.

THE RELENTLESS FORCE OF FAITH

Faith, when truly felt and understood, is not a quiet acceptance but a powerful Divine Feminine force carrying us through the maze of life. Faith is the embodiment of divine persistence—a companion whispering encouragement when your internal and external world is loud with doubt. She doesn't wait for us to have everything all figured out as she invites us to step boldly into the unknown with nothing more than the belief that we are capable of navigating whatever is put in front of us.

Faith is relentless in nature, not because she guarantees success at everything but because she's asking us to show up with unwavering trust, even when doubt and disbelief cling to us like a shadow. Faith urges us to move, to act, to push forward despite not seeing the full picture of what will happen. She's a continuous choice of your free will—a conscious commitment to keep walking when the road twists unexpectedly and the terrain grows rough and treacherous. Unlike fleeting hope or passive optimism, Faith commands us to be a participant in how our journey unfolds.

Choosing Faith in moments of doubt is not an easy task. It's a dance between trust and fear, where the music of life tests our willingness to believe in what cannot be touched or seen. When life is unpredictable and the future feels like a blank canvas, painted only in shades of uncertainty, Faith is a gentle muse urging us to pick up the brush and trust the strokes we choose.

According to Faith, every step taken is a declaration: *I will not be paralyzed by what I cannot control. I will move forward, knowing that I am guided by a force stronger than doubt. I will walk with Faith. I do not yield.*

The power of Faith is the strongest when our logical minds falter. The analytical part of us seeks proof, the tangible signs that everything will work before taking a step. But the energy of Faith requires you to transcend the limitations of the mind and listen instead to the whispers of your intuition, the gentle nudges that guide you when reason provides no answers. This type of trust asks that we honor our inner knowing, that sacred voice that encourages us to breathe through discomfort and lean in to life's mysteries.

Faith is more than resilience; she's the embodiment of surrender paired with action.

She's the essence of divine timing—comforting you while actively teaching you how to ebb and flow. She teaches you that while you may not control every moment of your life, if you keep moving, keep floating from moment to moment, you will eventually learn how to fly.

One of Faith's most challenging invitations for growth is to remain steady when nothing else is. To be the calm in the storm, even when everything has been swept away. In these moments it's hard to believe in the good if you focus on everything around you. This is where Faith moves from an abstract idea to a force felt deep in your soul—a relentless energy that doesn't allow you to collapse under the weight of uncertainty.

Faith asks that your strength isn't measured by your ability to avoid fear but your willingness to feel it and keep going anyway. This energy doesn't ask us to suppress fear or pretend we haven't had doubts. Instead, she asks that we acknowledge them, breathe through them and keep moving when there is fear. The act of choosing Faith over fear doesn't mean we have all the answers or that we always feel confident, because we don't. It means that you are willing to trust the answers will come exactly when you need them, and that confidence is an energy you cultivate by stepping forward. Confidence never comes first.

Faith shows up in the quiet moments . . . the ones where the world is still but your mind is not. The times where the mind races and sleep feels far off and the worries of the world echo in the silence, she's still there. She's whispering that while you may not be able to see how—everything is working out.

To walk with Faith is to embody the knowledge that life's journey is not a straight path or one without challenges. You are asked to understand that obstacles are not barriers but opportunities to embody more trust, growth, and connection. Faith does not eliminate risk or pain, but she does teach you that you have what it takes to navigate both with more ease. Each time you choose to believe and act on those beliefs, you strengthen your connection with your highest, most authentic self and all the unseen forces supporting you along the way.

The force of Faith asks for your participation—calling you to make bold choices, to trust in your ability to adapt, and let go of the need for guarantees when taking action. Faith will not promise you an easy road, but she will make sure you have what you need to walk it. And through that promise, that bargain with Faith, you access the strength to keep walking even when the road ahead is hidden from view and you are very, very tired.

As we move forward, Faith wants you to know that you are more capable than you realize. You can manifest a life more beautiful, joyful, and fulfilling than your analytical mind understands is possible, and all you have to do is believe what your soul already knows to be true.

ALIGNING WITH HIGHER PURPOSE

Faith isn't a passive presence in your life; she's a powerful compass, guiding you toward your higher purpose. She's an unwavering reminder that your path is not random but intricately woven with intention. When you learn to align with Faith's compass, you move forward not just with blind, faltering hope but with clarity and intention that stems from deep within you. This alignment requires you to see Faith as more than just your trust in Source; it's also an act of moving toward your highest alignment by trusting yourself. It's a recognition that we are not just observers of our life's path but active participants equipped with everything we need to navigate it.

The energy of Faith's compass lies in her ability to shift our perspective from seeking proof to cultivating belief. When we look outside ourselves for constant validation or certainty, we miss the gentle nudges Faith offers us to realign with our purpose. She teaches us that we don't need to see the entire map before taking a step; rather, we need to trust that our inner knowing will reveal what we need, in divine timing exactly when we need it. This is not an easy lesson to learn—especially for those of us conditioned to rely on logic and tangible evidence. But it is a vital one. Faith asks that we shift from waiting on external circumstances to being led by a whispering knowing that says, "You are on the right path, even if it doesn't all make sense right now."

Aligning with a higher purpose through Faith means allowing yourself to be guided by intuition, dreams, and the soft whispers of insight that arise when you quiet your mind. It's in these moments, when we let go of overthinking and analyzing, that Faith gently directs us, saying, "This is your path. Trust it." Your higher purpose becomes clearer not through force but through attunement—an openness to listen, to adjust, and to follow where Faith is leading you, even when the route is obscured by life's uncertainty. This alignment demands patience. Faith doesn't operate on the timelines of the analytical mind; she works within the vast expanse of divine timing, where every experience contributes to your greater understanding of yourself and the world around you.

One of the most profound shifts that Faith brings is the understanding that we must surrender control to embrace true alignment with our highest, most authentic self.

So often, fear tricks us into thinking that we need to manage every detail of our lives to ensure safety or success. This fear-based approach leaves us exhausted, perpetually grasping for control that was never ours to begin with. But Faith invites you to release this false sense of security. She reminds you that surrendering is not giving up—it's giving over control. It's releasing the tight grip on outcomes and trusting that you are the co-creators of your life. When we learn to dance and ebb and flow with Source we find the rhythm of our authenticity.

Surrendering doesn't mean you're left powerless or resigned to fate. It's quite the opposite. It's an act of courage, an empowered choice to participate in life with an open heart, unburdened by the chains of needing to know *how* everything will play out. *This type of surrender is where Faith's true power is revealed: in the ability to walk into the unknown with a grounded sense of trust.* Surrendering control creates space for flow and divine timing to operate in your life. It invites you to experience life with less resistance and more harmony, knowing that even unexpected detours are not missteps but redirections that guide you on your highest, most aligned path of growth.

Contrasting surrender with control reveals how different your life unfolds with each energy. Your attempts to control every aspect of your journey come from a place of fear—the fear of the unknown, of failure, of disappointment. These attempts lead to stress, rigidity, and an inability to pivot when life becomes unpredictable and throws you off course. In contrast, aligning with Faith and surrendering control opens you up to freedom. You become lighter, more adaptable, and more connected to the magic of life.

The very act of releasing the illusion of control becomes a declaration that you trust the path and trust yourself to walk it, no matter what challenges appear.

Faith's compass teaches us to recognize that our higher purpose is less about a fixed destination and more about the ongoing act of alignment. We often think of purpose as a singular event or a revelation that will arrive fully formed. However, Faith shows us that our purpose is continuously being refined, shaped by our choices and experiences, and the moments when we allow ourselves to listen to our inner guidance. This understanding shifts your focus from an anxiety-driven search for "what's next" to a peaceful acceptance that your path will reveal itself one step at a time. And with each step taken with Faith, you deepen your trust in both the unseen forces guiding you and in your own ability to keep going.

When you align with Faith, you also strengthen your trust in yourself. This is perhaps one of Faith's most overlooked gifts: the empowerment that comes from realizing that you are worthy of the journey you are on. To align with Faith is to affirm that your inner voice holds wisdom worth following, even when it challenges conventional logic. It's a recognition that the universe doesn't just work through external signs, synchronicities, and cosmic alignments but through your choices, desires, and beliefs. By trusting in yourself, you follow Faith and allow her to illuminate a path that is uniquely yours . . . one that reflects who you really are.

The beauty of aligning with your higher purpose through Faith is that it encourages you to tune in to the deeper truths of your existence. You come to understand that your purpose is not defined by a single achievement or moment but by the continuous act of becoming—becoming more aware, more authentic, and more attuned to the divine calling within you. Faith, as your compass, empowers you to move forward with this understanding, allowing you to be intentional with your choices and aligned in your actions. She asks you to show up in each moment with an open heart, a grounded spirit, and the belief that you are walking a path uniquely designed for you.

Surrendering doesn't eliminate life's challenges, but it reframes them. You come to see obstacles not as insurmountable barriers but as opportunities for growth. These challenges become a part of the dance with Source, teaching you resilience, humility, and the courage to adapt. The act of surrendering frees you from the exhaustion of control, creating room for possibilities you couldn't have imagined when bounded by fear.

Faith reminds us that the unknown holds not just potential hardship but also potential joy, success, and fulfillment.

Ultimately, Faith's compass teaches and transforms the way we live. We begin to see that every challenge, triumph, and breath is part of a larger story—a story that isn't about getting to a destination but about who you become along the way. With Faith, you learn to release the fears that hold you back and embrace the trust that propels you forward.

In doing so, you find that your higher purpose is not only something to be discovered but something to be lived—moment by moment, step by step, aligned with the flow of divine guidance and timing available to you.

OUR BARGAIN WITH FAITH

Accepting the bargain with Faith is a practice that requires trust in both Source and in ourselves. This dual trust forms the foundation of a balanced and aligned life, where spiritual beliefs and personal agency co-exist in harmony. Faith, in her purest form, invites us to recognize that we are not just passive recipients of divine intervention but active participants who shape our path through choices grounded in both surrender and responsibility.

Trusting Source means acknowledging that a higher intelligence orchestrates our experiences with purpose and wisdom. This bargain asks us to look beyond the immediacy of our circumstances and accept that life is unfolding in ways we might not fully understand. When you lean in to this trust, you move through life with an openness that dissolves resistance. Faith teaches us that Source is not detached from our struggles or successes; rather, it is intricately connected to every heartbeat, every breath, guiding us when we cannot see the path clearly. This trust in Source becomes an anchor when doubt arises, a silent assurance that whispers, "You are held, you are seen, and you are exactly where you need to be."

Accepting the bargain with Faith extends far beyond placing your confidence solely in the unseen. It requires an equally strong trust in yourself—your ability to navigate the complexities of life with courage, intuition, and resilience. This is where many get cold feet; self-trust is often more challenging than trusting in the divine. Faith calls you to believe not only in the guidance of Source but also in your own capacity to respond to that guidance. It is an inner knowing that says, "I am capable of facing whatever comes my way, not because I have all the answers but because I am aligned with truth."

Trusting yourself means embracing your imperfections and understanding that missteps are not failures but valuable lessons. The bargain with Faith is not a promise of a life without challenges; rather, it's an assurance that you can make it through anything with divine support and aligning your inner strength and wisdom with your highest, most authentic self. It's a practice of leaning in to uncertainty, not with reckless abandon but with the confidence that you have the tools to adapt, learn, and grow. This acceptance of trust in Source and self allows you to move forward with grounded assurance, rooted in the understanding that both forces are at play in the unfolding of your journey.

The balance between trusting in a higher power and taking responsibility for our actions is one of the most delicate aspects of Faith.

Spiritual surrender does not absolve us from participating in the creation of our reality; rather, it requires that we meet Source halfway. Walking with Faith is not a passive surrender to fate; it's an active, engaged relationship with the divine and with ourselves. You must be willing to show up, make decisions, and act in ways that align with your higher purpose, especially when the outcome is uncertain. This interplay between surrender and action is where Faith reveals her power.

Self-trust inherently comes with responsibility. When we trust ourselves, we acknowledge that we are co-creators of our destiny, holding the power to shape our experiences through intention and action. *Faith, then, becomes a catalyst for accountability.* She asks that you take ownership of your choices, knowing that each decision you make contributes to the unfolding of your path. This responsibility is not a burden but a sacred duty that honors our role as co-creator with Source.

Faith affirms that while we may not control every outcome, we have a say in how we show up.

She asks us to step into this role willingly, understanding that our commitment to take inspired action is met with divine support. Accepting Faith also means learning to navigate the tension between surrender and effort.

There will be times when life's circumstances test your resolve, challenging you to maintain your trust in Source while also asking you if there's an action you can take. It's in these moments where Faith becomes a bridge between your spiritual beliefs and the tangible reality of your daily life. Surrendering to divine timing does not mean relinquishing your power; it means trusting that when you act from a place of alignment, you are supported. The energy of Faith asks us to transform surrender into an empowering practice that blends our acceptance of what is with taking steps toward the future we want. Faith asks that we slow down and ask ourselves, "What step is next?"

Faith encourages you to find equilibrium between leaning on Source and leaning in to your own strength.

This duality is our world: We are both led and leaders, both guided and guides. Both . . . and. Faith is not one-dimensional; she is multilayered, existing in the space where trust, action, surrender, and accountability merge. This integration requires a nuanced understanding that you can ask for signs, guidance, and assistance from Source, but you must also be willing to listen to the answers and take the next step, even when it feels uncertain, when hard choices have to be made. Faith compels us to do our part, to participate fully and with integrity—co-creators of our experience.

Through this bargain with Faith, we learn that our trust in Source and trust in ourselves are not mutually exclusive but intertwined. Each supports and strengthens the other, creating a cycle of confidence and surrender that propels us forward. On one hand, the more we trust Source's guidance, the more we believe in our ability to interpret and act on that guidance. And on the other, the more we act from a place of inner trust, the deeper our belief in the divine becomes. Infinitely intertwined—quantumly connected and entangled.

Inviting Faith into your daily life means living in a way that honors both divine guidance and personal effort. It's the quiet confidence that you're capable of handling whatever comes, not because you are infallible but because you trust in the relationship between yourself and the divine. This relationship is a partnership, where Source provides opportunities and direction, and you provide the willingness to engage, learn, and evolve. The beauty of this entanglement is it allows you to move through life with a sense of wholeness—anchored in both surrender and action, alignment and effort, belief, and courage.

Ultimately, accepting the bargain with Faith means living in alignment with a higher truth: that we are never alone in our journey but neither are we without the power to influence it.

You are being guided, and you are capable of responding to that guidance with the fullness of who you are. This bargain empowers you to live authentically, to take responsibility for your life, and to surrender to the flow of Source with your heart open to the future.

FAITH'S ROLE IN OVERCOMING CHALLENGES

Challenges are an inevitable part of the journey. They arrive uninvited, testing our beliefs and shaking the foundations on which we stand. It's in these moments that Faith steps forward, not as a protector that promises to prevent hardship but as a wise and patient teacher who helps us navigate through them. Faith shows up to remind us that while we may not have control over life's lessons, we have control over how we choose to meet them. In the depths of difficulty, Faith whispers that your greatest growth comes from your willingness to confront what you'd rather avoid. She teaches us that challenges are not detours or delays but essential stops on our path to becoming who we are meant to be.

The power of Faith is in her ability to guide you through uncertainty.

When life veers into chaos and doubt creeps in, Faith asks you to look beyond the immediate discomfort and trust in the greater purpose behind the struggle. She shows you that difficult times are not a sign of abandonment or punishment by Source but an invitation to deepen your relationship with yourself and your Creator. It's in these moments that Faith takes on her most powerful role—not as a tool to bypass our pain but a relentless force empowering us to face it with Grace.

When we approach challenges with Faith, we start to see them less as adversarial moments and more as key teachers. Each challenge holds within it the potential to refine and fortify our energy. Faith teaches us to stay present with discomfort and to trust in our ability to rise again, no matter how many times we fall. She reminds us strength is not measured by an absence of struggle but by our capacity to keep moving forward regardless of it.

When the steps on the path aren't clear and you feel like there's no solution in sight, walking with Faith requires that you believe a solution is showing up in perfect timing.

Resilience, forged by your bargain with Faith, enables you to transform obstacles into stepping stones. Faith teaches you to trust that every challenge carries a lesson and every setback holds the opportunity for growth. This perspective does not minimize the pain of hardship but repositions it as part of a larger narrative—one in which our spirit is shaped, refined, and prepared for greater things. *Challenges become opportunities to cultivate an unyielding trust that life, despite its uncertainties, is working in our favor.* It is an exercise in consistent trust, one that asks you to remain unwavering, even when faced with circumstances that seem insurmountable.

Consistent trust is a deep-rooted conviction that even in the most difficult of events, there's meaning, and even when the outcomes do not match our expectations, there's purpose to it all. Trust does not ignore the reality of suffering or the weight of disappointment. Rather, it acknowledges these experiences while holding on to the simple truth that there is something greater at play. Faith urges us to dig deeper when life tests us, to find our inner knowing that we will not be defined by any one moment alone.

She also asks that we not only endure but actively engage with the situation, encouraging us to search for the insight offered. The lesson of patience, the reminder of humility, and the realization of our own resilience is taught. No moment is wasted. Each challenge contributing to a more complete understanding of who we are and what we are capable of.

With Faith, we see resilience not as a trait reserved for the extraordinary but a practice cultivated by those willing to trust.

It's in the everyday acts of holding on when we're tempted to let go—the moments we choose joy instead of despair. Faith reminds us that this, too, is part of your becoming.

Faith's role in overcoming challenges extends beyond individual moments of hardship, weaving through the fabric of our lives, shaping how we respond to life as a whole. Faith invites you to reframe your narrative—from one where life happens *to* you to one where life happens *for* you. This shift empowers you to see adversity not as evidence of failure but as proof of your capacity to navigate life with courage and Grace. Faith then becomes a bridge between struggle and meaning, connecting the two and transforming our perspective.

Living with this kind of Faith doesn't mean we won't encounter moments where doubt makes an appearance or where the weight of our challenges feels unbearable. But it does mean that within those moments, there is an anchor that holds you steady—a trust that even when you can't yet make sense of the pieces, you know they are forming a picture greater than you can see. Faith's lesson is that, in the journey of overcoming, you are not only surviving but also evolving into a deeper, more aware version of yourself.

Resilience paired with Faith teaches us that moving through challenges isn't about proving our invincibility but embracing our humanity. It's about accepting that we will experience pain, uncertainty, and moments of fear, but within those moments, we are held by an energy that transcends logic. It's an energy that tells us that beyond our conscious understanding, we are being guided, and that guidance, whether subtle or loud, is present for every step we take.

Ultimately, Faith calls you to rise above the immediate and get a better look at the big picture. She asks you to choose trust in the process, even when the process feels awful. When challenges arise, let Faith be your guide, leading you deeper into your purpose. Faith is the steady hand lifting you from simply enduring life to truly embracing it.

SIGNS AND SYNCHRONICITIES FROM FAITH

Faith's language transcends words—we find her messages in the subtle, yet powerful, synchronicities that appear when we need them most. These divine messages are given in the moments that feel too perfect to be coincidences. They're moments that feel like Source leans in and whispers, "*You are exactly where you need to be. You've got this. Keep going.*" These signs are Faith's way of reminding you that you are not alone. She's showing you that, despite your fears and uncertainties, you are guided and supported in every moment.

Recognizing these signs requires a shift in awareness—a willingness to look beyond the surface and listen with your inner knowing first. It's Faith that asks you to trust your intuition when logic doesn't provide any answers. We've all had moments where a song plays just as we need to hear it, where a friend reaches out in the exact moment we feel alone, and repeating number patterns show up when we're questioning our path. *None of it is random.* It's Faith leaving messages of support. Nudges to keep going. These experiences may seem ordinary to the unawakened eye, but to those aligned with Faith, they're anything but. They're the signs leading us back to trust, reassurances we're seen and heard by something greater than our understanding.

These signs show us how much beauty can be woven into our daily lives through their simplicity.

A synchronistic moment with a stranger who shares the exact message we needed to hear in the moment we needed to hear it. A feather appearing just as we're contemplating a difficult decision, signaling we're supported and aligned with the choice we're making. Simple but synchronistic moments confirm your thoughts and feelings the second you have them. These divinely timed moments happen when we're at the crossroads of our lives, when uncertainty and fear threaten to shake our resolve. Faith not only illuminates these signs but also encourages us to pause, reflect, and take in the deeper meaning they offer.

Building trust in intuitive guidance over the analytical mind requires a softening of control—a willingness to believe in what we cannot see and accepting that Source's way of communicating with us often defies conventional logic. Faith invites you to shift from seeking tangible evidence to embracing an intuitive knowing that reassures you without needing "objective" proof. When we learn to trust these divine nudges, we start to see the world through a new perspective. The line between coincidence and intentionality begins to blur, replaced by an awareness that life is not a series of isolated events but a deeply connected web of meaning and purpose.

Faith reminds us that we are on the right path, even when it doesn't feel like it. The signs and synchronicities become trail markers, guiding the way even when the path's direction has become unclear. When we face a challenge and ask for guidance, answers appear in an unexpected way—a book falls off a shelf with the message we need, a dream playing out the very answer to the question we asked. The options for delivery are endless, simple, and flow naturally into our awareness with a gentleness that has the analytical mind questioning if we received the answer or if it was mere coincidence. These experiences serve as confirmation that, in fact, we are being guided by forces greater than our own will.

These signs show you that when you walk with Faith, she'll illuminate each step exactly when it's needed.

These confirmations aren't usually grand gestures; they're found in the smallest of interactions—the mundane, in-between moments of your life. The moments where a breeze seems to hold a whisper, where a tree appears to wave, and the sun breaks through clouds, revealing a silver lining. Faith asks you to pay attention, to slow down enough to see and feel these moments, rooting in a deeper sense of peace. The more you tune in to the signs and synchronicity being shared with you, the more you strengthen your connection with Faith, inviting her presence as a constant energy in your life.

There are times when fear and doubt try to drown out Faith, and in those moments, signs and synchronicities become something more—they become lifelines to your Creator. When fear screams and there are more questions than answers, Faith asks you to find your center and remain open. She asks you to get quiet and listen for the subtle messages that show you the universe is still working on your behalf.

Faith empowers you to find meaning in your moments.

To walk with Faith is to trust that these signs are not just figments of your imagination but the quiet connections to Source. They're your validations from Source. Trusting these signs means you surrender the urge to second-guess their significance and choose instead to embrace them as beautiful gifts. Recognizing these nods from Source will fill you with gratitude, evolving your vibration and connecting you to your frequency. Each one a testament that Faith is always working quietly, guiding you through the unknown.

Faith is an active, dynamic, and powerful force that we can engage with daily. Faith's quiet resolve in the face of uncertainty is a steady presence reassuring you when the path ahead feels hidden. To invite Faith in is to commit to feeling her in your greatest moments of need and in the gentle ebb and flow of everyday life. She is the stillness reminding us that every moment carries a promise of learning and growth.

Faith asks for your participation, asking you to make a conscious choice to lean in to trust even when the evidence is sparse. She challenges you to step beyond your comfort zones, to take leaps that defy logic, and to trust that each step forward is met with support, even if unseen. Faith goes beyond the well-lit places of our world, entering the depths where there is no joy and illuminates the darkness. Walking with Faith is a choice to anchor yourself in trust, believing that you are guided and held, even as life shifts and changes dramatically around you.

Challenges, once viewed as obstacles, become opportunities on this walk with Faith. With each one faced and overcome, we deepen our understanding of how her compass leads to our highest, most authentic expression. She transforms setbacks into setups for greater strength and growth, shaping you into a version of yourself that faces unpredictability with Grace.

Faith teaches you that adversity is an invitation to evolve.

Living with Faith requires a shift in your perspective: from seeing life as happening to you to understanding that life happens for you. Faith provides the energetic bridge connecting your experiences to the deeper meaning of your life, allowing you to live with purpose.

There will be moments where you question the steps on your journey, where the weight of it all feels overwhelming and the light at the end of the tunnel seems dim. Yet, even in those moments, Faith remains. She reminds you that even when you lack understanding, you can trust your life is unfolding as it should.

Faith assures you that we are all an important piece of a bigger puzzle—more beautiful and complex than we could ever imagine.

Let her guide you, support you, and remind you that you are always exactly where you need to be.

You've got this. Keep going.

CHAPTER 3

THE DARK FOREST

Imagine standing at the edge of a vast, shadowy forest. Its boundaries are unclear, and the path forward isn't marked. Entering the forest equals stepping into a transformation process that is completely unknown, yet there's a tug to enter. This is the Dark Forest—the space we must enter to awaken. It's a place of mystery and challenge, where the light seems distant and every step forward is uncertain. To reclaim the truth of who we are, we must enter the forest.

Life's most powerful transformations begin with a journey into the unknown. The Dark Forest, while unfamiliar, is a sacred space where our beliefs and behaviors dissolve, making way for growth. The wildness of this uncharted territory can hurt at times, as we are forced to process and transform dense and powerful experiences. But this journey is the bargain we make for growth—a means to rediscover our light through the shadows.

The darkness of the forest isn't an indication of evil or mistaken direction. It's the space where our highest alignment is created. In its stillness, we are called to release the noise of life and attune to something deeper: the pull of our soul's purpose. This alignment doesn't come without challenge. As we strip away illusions, confront fears, and release attachments to what we know, we make space for transformation. The discomfort of walking in the dark allows us to remember our true potential and begin aligning with the highest version of ourselves.

This journey requires courage—a willingness to face the unknown, to let go of what isn't serving us, and to trust in the process even when we can't see the way forward. Courage also comes from trusting in unseen guidance—the whispers of intuition and the gentle nudges from something greater guiding us step by step. It's through this process of surrender that we uncover our strength.

The path of the Dark Forest is one of initiation. It's an invitation to step into a higher understanding of ourselves and our connection to the greater whole. Like a caterpillar dissolving into goo before emerging as a beautiful butterfly, we too must undergo a complete metamorphosis. The darkness is not the end; it's the portal to something greater. Every misstep, every challenge becomes a teacher, redirecting us toward alignment with our soul's purpose.

Growth is a sacred exchange—a bargain between who you are and who you are becoming. It's not a struggle to avoid but a process to embrace. When we resist, the forest becomes a place of confusion and despair. But when we lean in, accepting the forest as part of our journey, it becomes a place of discovery, healing, and deep transformation.

As we move through this chapter, we'll reframe your relationship with the darkness, seeing it not as an enemy but as a teacher who moves you toward the light. Awakening is promised within the Dark Forest but only if you have the courage to enter. Every shadow you encounter holds the reflection of light. Walk with curiosity and courage. Healing and awakening aren't about avoiding the dark—it's discovering who you are within it.

UNDERSTANDING THE DARK FOREST

The Dark Forest isn't just a metaphor for the challenges of awakening; it's a mirror, reflecting both the depths of our struggles and the brilliance of our potential. Unlike familiar paths we can walk with certainty, the forest is uncharted, raw, and filled with the unknown. Its shadows conceal our deepest truths, waiting to be rediscovered.

The confusion, fear, and disconnection we feel in this space aren't signs of failure—they're the natural byproducts of stepping out of the comfort of who we've always believed ourselves to be. Even when we're discontent with life, change rarely feels easy at first. Awakening isn't a straightforward path either; it's messy and disorienting by design. But disorientation is essential. It's the soul's way of stripping away outdated frameworks—the thoughts, beliefs, and patterns that no longer serve our growth.

The darkness of the forest isn't a punishment—it's an invitation to meet the parts of yourself you've long ignored. The wounds that surface aren't here to harm you; they're here to be seen, understood, and healed. The energies that rise within you—unprocessed pain, limiting beliefs, and old narratives—have shaped your reality up to this point. The forest demands you confront these truths, bringing presence and compassion to what you've previously denied.

The Dark Forest is a universal experience, though it goes by many names. Some call it a pilgrimage; others know it as the dark night of the soul. I'm guided to share that it's all of the above. The forest holds a darkness that can feel endless as we traverse unfamiliar territory with no clear destination in sight. Yet no matter what form the forest takes, this journey is required for transformation. Every soul walking the path of awakening will face their own version of it.

For some, the forest may take the shape of grief—peeling away layers of loss to uncover a deeper understanding of love. For others, it might appear as the collapse of an identity, forcing them to rebuild from a foundation of authenticity. Whatever form the forest takes, it asks for trust in the process—especially when the way forward is impossible to see.

The terrain of the forest is both internal and external. Internally, it reveals the fears, doubts, and beliefs that shape how we see the world. Externally, it manifests in circumstances that challenge us—relationships that test our boundaries, careers that no longer align, or events that shake our stability. Each of these divinely orchestrated moments serves as a lantern on the path, leading us closer to the truth of who we are.

The forest teaches through contrast. In navigating the dark, we come to recognize the light—not as an abstract concept but as a deeply felt experience. The forest strips away what you think you know to uncover the energy of who you are. It compels you to ask the questions you've avoided: Who am I without achievements, roles, or attachments? What do I truly value? What is my purpose?

Darkness is a teacher unlike any other. It doesn't coddle or soften the edges of the truth to spare our feelings. Instead, it demands honesty, even when it's uncomfortable. The lessons we receive here are forged through our lived experience, not theory. The forest also creates sacred space for pause, reflection, and realignment. In this stillness, you learn to trust the process. Resistance only prolongs the journey, while acceptance unlocks the doors.

The Dark Forest is a rite of passage—the proving ground for the soul's evolution. Walk with Faith. In this space, you learn to embrace uncertainty, find strength in surrender, and transform the darkness from an enemy into an ally. Each shadow holds a piece of the light you are destined to reclaim.

THE FLAMES OF AWAKENING

Just as a natural forest uses fire to regenerate—burning away the underbrush and dead trees no longer in the energy of growth—we too must burn away the layers that hold us back from our highest expression. The flames crack open our seeds of potential, setting our souls on fire.

Every fire starts with a spark, a catalyst for change, and our awakenings are no different. It could be the devastating loss of a loved one, the collapse of a relationship, or the unraveling of a career or identity we thought would last forever. It might even be the unbearable weight of waking up one day to a question that shakes us to our core: Is this really my life? Whatever the spark, it rarely feels like a gentle nudge toward transformation. Instead, it ignites an inferno within us. Every cell in our body screams in the face of it. It tears through the familiar, leaving nothing untouched.

Standing at the edge of this force, we watch everything we've known slip through our fingertips. The life we built, the roles we played, the identity we wore—all of it feels fragile, crumbling under the intensity of the awakening. There's grief in this moment, a deep mourning for the person we once were, even if that version of ourselves never truly felt aligned or happy. And yet, even in that grief, there is something else. Beneath the chaos and pain, there is a whisper—faint but undeniable: *This is not the end. This is the beginning.*

The breakdowns that follow feel relentless, as the fire consumes everything in its path. Emotionally, we unravel. Waves of grief, fear, and anger crash over us, often without warning. One moment, we are functioning; the next, we're sobbing uncontrollably in the car or lying awake at 3 A.M., unable to see a way forward. Mentally, the stories we've clung to about who we are and how the world works no longer make sense. Spiritually, you may feel untethered, adrift in a void where the divine presence you once trusted feels distant or absent. It feels as though everything is falling apart.

But here's the truth: In falling apart, you are being made whole.

The flames of awakening are not here to destroy you—they are here to burn away all that is not truly who you are. They clear the way for you to rise from the ashes as your most authentic self. The flames devour the illusions you've clung to, the masks you've worn, and the fears that have kept you small. And yes, it hurts. It hurts to face the parts of ourselves we've buried. It hurts to release the life we thought we wanted. But this pain is sacred. It doesn't destroy—it transforms.

Surrendering to the flames is the hardest lesson we'll ever face. We fight because fighting feels safer. We cling to the ashes of what was because letting go feels like losing control. But resistance only deepens the suffering. Surrender, on the other hand, is an act of divine courage. It is standing in the fire and saying, "I don't understand this, but I'm willing to trust it." Surrender allows the fire to work its magic, even when you don't yet know what will remain when the flames subside.

And when you surrender, something extraordinary happens. The breakdowns—the sleepless nights, the tears, the moments of despair—begin to reveal their purpose. The losses create space. The grief softens into wisdom. The confusion begins to clear, offering glimpses of truth. The fire doesn't destroy; it purifies. It clears the way for something new, something authentic to emerge.

This is the alchemy of awakening. Breaking down is not a failure; it is a sacred dismantling. It's the soul's way of clearing out the old—the outdated beliefs, limiting roles, and patterns that no longer serve you—so you can rebuild on a foundation of truth, of authenticity. These moments of collapse, though painful, are acts of Grace. They remind you that you are not here to live a life of half-truths and compromises. You are here to live fully and authentically, and that requires burning away all that is false.

Moving through the flames shows you a resilience you didn't know you had. The fire pushes you to the very edge of what you think you can bear, only to show you that you can go farther. It reveals a strength we never knew existed. It teaches us that beginnings are born from endings. Every tear shed, every belief questioned, every piece of the old self released serves a purpose. All of it is guiding you toward the truest, most aligned version of yourself.

Awakening is a fire that sparks the light you carry within. Walk through the flames with courage. Yes, they will burn, but they will not destroy you. They will transform you. You will rise from the ashes—raw, unshakable, and original.

NAVIGATING THE DARKNESS

The Dark Forest tests every fiber of your being. It asks you to let go of the life you've outgrown, step into the unknown, and trust that you'll find your way—even when the path feels invisible. Though it often feels as if we're fumbling in the dark, we're not navigating empty-handed. Within you, you carry tools powerful enough to light the way: your intuition, self-reflection, trust, and most importantly Faith. These are not just survival tools; they are energies of transformation, reshaping how you move through the forest and who you become on the other side.

1. Learn to Trust Your Inner Compass

In the absence of clear directions, your intuition becomes your inner compass, guiding you when nothing else seems to make sense. Intuition isn't always logical; in fact, it often defies the structure and predictability your analytical mind craves. It doesn't come with step-by-step instructions or neat conclusions. Instead, it's the quiet pull in your gut, the gentle nudge of your heart, or the inexplicable sense that one path feels right, even if you can't explain why.

Learning to trust your intuition requires patience and practice.

Many of us are conditioned to override it, dismissing it as irrational or unimportant. But intuition isn't random; it's deeply rooted in wisdom that transcends conscious thought. It's the language of the soul, communicating through feelings, symbols, and subtle impressions. The more you listen, the louder it becomes.

Self-reflection creates the space to connect with this inner compass. Journaling, for instance, is one of the most accessible tools for this process. When you put pen to paper, you bypass the chatter of the conscious mind and tap into deeper truths. Try writing without judgment, letting your thoughts flow freely. *What patterns emerge? What emotions rise to the surface?* These are often the whispers of intuition, waiting to be acknowledged. And if you don't like journaling, I get it. I didn't either, until the commitment to the practice completely changed my life. Move through the uncomfortability of letting your thoughts flow.

Meditation is another key to unlocking the wisdom of your intuition. In stillness, you learn to differentiate between the noise of fear and the calm certainty of inner knowing. A consistent meditation practice teaches you to sit with uncertainty without rushing to fill the void with answers. It creates a deeper connection to yourself and fosters the trust you need to follow your intuition, even when the path ahead is unclear.

When you commit to strengthening your intuitive connection, something remarkable happens: You stop seeking validation from external sources. You no longer rely on the world to tell you who you are or what you should do. Instead, you begin to trust the quiet certainty within you, knowing that it will guide you toward what is most aligned with your higher self.

2. Allow Faith to Be the Light That Leads You

If intuition is the compass, Faith is the light that pierces the darkness. Faith doesn't promise the absence of fear or doubt; she's the vibration that encourages the decision to move forward despite them. There's always a purpose to the chaos, even when we can't see it yet.

Faith asks us to trust not only in Source but also in ourselves. Faith's frequency is the delicate balance between surrendering to divine guidance and taking responsibility for your choices and actions. In the forest, where every step feels uncertain, this duality becomes essential. Faith reminds you that you're co-creators of your reality. It's not about sitting back and waiting for answers to fall into your lap. It's about showing up, taking action, and trusting that Source will meet you in the space between action and manifestation.

Maintaining a connection with Faith isn't always easy to sustain. In the face of prolonged uncertainty, the connection can feel fragile, like a flickering flame struggling against the wind. This is where gratitude and affirmation become invaluable. They nurture the connection with Faith, strengthening your link with the divine, reminding you that you're never walking this path alone.

One of the most transformative aspects of Faith is her ability to reframe your relationship with fear. Fear thrives in the shadows of the unknown, whispering stories of worst-case scenarios and failure. But Faith whispers a different story: one of trust, resilience, and purpose. She transforms fear into fuel, propelling you forward when everything in you wants to retreat.

3. Trust the Process

Patience is perhaps one of the most consistent lessons the forest teaches us. When we're in the midst of darkness, we want answers. We want clarity. We want to know when—or if—we'll reach the other side. But the forest doesn't work on our timeline. Transformation is a process, not an event. The seeds of change we plant don't sprout overnight.

Trusting the process means allowing clarity to emerge in its own time. It means resisting the urge to force outcomes and instead surrender to the flow of life. This doesn't mean you stop taking action. It means you take inspired action, guided by your intuition and alignment with Faith, while releasing attachment to specific results.

Practical tools can help you cultivate this mindset. Mindfulness practices, for example, teach you to focus on the present moment rather than getting lost in the uncertainty of the future. When fear of the unknown arises, bring yourself back to the now. *What do you know to be true in this moment? What small step can you take today?*

Nature, too, can be a powerful teacher in this regard. Spend time outside, observing the rhythm of the natural world. Notice how the seasons change without resistance, how rivers carve paths over time, how trees stand tall through storms. The forest may feel endless, but it operates within the same laws of life: cycles of destruction and renewal, endings and beginnings.

Navigating the darkness isn't about eliminating discomfort; it's about learning to hold space for it.

Journaling, gratitude, mindfulness, and meditation remain some of the most practical tools for this work, but they are far from the only ones. Breath work, for example, is a simple yet profound practice that helps you regulate your nervous system and move through fear with greater ease.

Use practices that resonate with you. Experiment with guided meditations, affirmations, or even creative outlets like painting or music. The goal isn't to avoid the darkness but to move through it with as much ease and presence as possible.

Every time you choose to trust your intuition, leaning in to Faith and releasing control, you're building resilience. The forest isn't meant to break you; it's meant to break down the illusions of this realm so that you can remember who you are. The tools we use and the mindset we cultivate aren't just survival mechanisms—they're acts of self-love. They remind you that, even in the darkest moments, you're worthy of care, compassion, and belief in your own light.

The journey through the forest is deeply personal, but it's not one you have to walk alone. Faith walks with you, guiding your steps. Your higher self lights the way. And with every tool you pick up, every act of surrender, and every moment of trust, you move closer to the truth of who you are.

The light you seek is already within you.

LESSONS FROM THE DARK FOREST

It feels important to reiterate the Dark Forest is not a punishment—it's an initiation, a sacred space where deep healing begins and transformation takes root. It's where the soul is called to strip away the masks it wears, to confront its rawest truths, and to rediscover the brilliance it has carried all along. The darkness isn't there to break you; it's there to remind you of your strength, your resilience, and the light that's been waiting for you all along.

The forest can feel merciless. It forces you to stand still when all you want to do is run. It pulls you into silence when you crave distractions to drown out your fear. But this stillness, this confrontation, is where the magic begins. In the quiet shadows, the soul speaks. It reminds you that no matter how lost you feel, the forest is not here to destroy you—it's here to deliver you back to yourself.

Each step through the darkness peels away a layer of illusion.

The fears that once seemed insurmountable start to shrink in the light of your awareness. You realize the narratives you've clung to—of unworthiness, failure, or despair—are nothing more than stories that you have the power to rewrite. The forest is not just a place of struggle; it's a forge where the soul is refined, where potential is shaped into purpose.

The transformation is quiet at first—like a faint ember catching flame. It's in the moment you decide to face what you've avoided. It's in the recognition that even in your most vulnerable state, you are still whole. Slowly, you begin to see what the forest is teaching you: that you are capable of holding both the pain of life's challenges and the beauty of your own unfolding.

Emerging from the Dark Forest is not simply leaving a difficult chapter behind—it's stepping into a new way of being. The world looks different, not because it has changed but because you have. Colors feel richer, the air lighter, and even the familiar has an unfamiliar vibrance to it. You carry with you a clarity pulled from the shadows—a profound understanding of who you are and what truly matters.

This emergence feels like reclaiming your power. The doubts that once controlled you no longer hold the same weight. You've faced your fears and emerged on the other side, not unscathed but stronger. And while the light feels like a homecoming, you carry a reverence for the darkness that shaped you.

You realize that the forest wasn't just a trial to endure but a teacher that revealed your potential.

The journey has rewired how you see yourself. You no longer feel the need to prove your worth because you know it is inherent. The forest teaches you to trust in your ability to navigate not only the light but also the shadow, with Grace and courage.

The greatest gift of the Dark Forest is the rediscovery of your light. It's easy to forget, in the chaos of life, that the light you seek has always been within you. The forest doesn't add anything to you; it clears away the noise and illusion, revealing the truth of your being.

This darkness becomes sacred when you embrace it. In its stillness, you reconnect with the pieces of yourself you've abandoned. You remember your capacity to heal, to grow, and to rise. The forest mirrors your strength back to you, and in its shadows, you begin to see not just what you've endured but what you're capable of becoming.

The forest doesn't promise an easy path. Its terrain is steep and its lessons relentless. But it offers something far more valuable: empowerment. It strips away what no longer serves you and leaves you with something unshakable—an intimate knowing of your own light and the wisdom to carry it forward.

> ***The light within you has never faltered, even in the darkest moments of this journey. This wasn't about finding the light; it was about remembering that it has always been yours.***

Emerging from the forest calls for celebration—not just of the light you've reclaimed but of the courage it took to walk through the darkness. Every tear, every stumble, every doubt was part of your becoming. You didn't just survive the forest; you allowed it to change you.

Now, as you stand in the light, you carry with you the sacred truth the forest taught you: that darkness is not the end of the story. It is the soil where growth begins. It is the canvas for your transformation.

The forest will stay with you—not as a shadow but as a reminder. Its lessons will guide you in the moments ahead when life feels heavy. It will remind you that no matter how dark the path becomes, your light is always enough to guide the way.

The forest didn't take you away from your journey—it *was* your journey. And it brought you here: to a place of alignment, clarity, and empowerment.

THE GUIDES WITHIN THE FOREST

The Dark Forest is a universal rite of passage that both humbles and empowers us. The stories of Isis, Hecate, and Quan Yin are beautiful mirrors of this journey, reminding us that wandering through the darkness is not where we are lost but where we are found. Their stories resonate because they are our stories—they are the blueprints for the soul's evolution.

Isis: The Power of Love and Creation

Isis was plunged into the raw pain of loss. Her partner Osiris was torn from her, dismembered, and scattered across realms; her world plunged into chaos. The grief was relentless—a suffocating darkness wrapped itself around her and her heart. But even in the depths of despair, Isis refused to surrender.

She embodied the vibration of Faith and stepped into the Dark Forest not with certainty but with a fierce determination to reclaim what was taken. Piece by piece, Isis scoured the realms, collecting the fragments of Osiris. Each piece she gathered was a testament to her embodiment of love, Faith, and her refusal to abandon the one who was entangled with her own soul. It was not an easy journey. The Dark Forest tested her resolve, forcing her to face her deepest fears and vulnerabilities.

When at last she had gathered all the pieces, Isis did not stop. She called upon the power within her, a force born of grief and devotion, and performed a miraculous act of creation through the void. With her magic, she resurrected Osiris, transforming death into life and despair into hope. Yet even this victory was bittersweet, as Osiris could no longer remain in the world of the living. His soul resurrected without a body.

Isis's journey through the Dark Forest teaches us that love is not just an emotion—it is a powerful energy that transcends loss. She reminds you that even when life feels shattered beyond repair, you hold within you the ability to gather the pieces and create something new. Her story is a beacon of resilience, showing you that the darkness can be a womb of creation, not a grave filled with despair.

Hecate: The Wisdom of the Crossroads

Hecate, the frequency of the crossroads, embodies the quiet power of the Dark Forest. She stands at the threshold of worlds, a guide through the unknown and a keeper of mysteries. Hecate's forest is not one of grief or loss but of choice—the liminal space where you are called to confront your fears and decide who you will become.

In the ancient stories, Hecate is often depicted holding torches, her light illuminating the way for those who are lost. But her light does not banish the shadows; it dances with them, showing only enough to take the next step. When Hecate illuminates the path, she does not give answers, only guidance of how to best navigate the crossroads, trusting you to find your own path.

In the Dark Forest, Hecate asks you to surrender your need for certainty and embrace the mystery of life. Her voice is a whisper in the silence, urging you to trust your intuition even when logic fails. She stands beside you in the darkest moments, her presence a reminder that you are never truly alone, even when the path ahead feels impossible to see.

Hecate's journey is one of empowerment. She shows us that the forest is not a place to be feared but a sacred space where we meet ourselves. Her torches are not a solution but an invitation—to step forward with courage, to trust the light within, and to honor the power of the choices you make in the dark.

Quan Yin: The Compassion of the Dark Forest

Quan Yin's story begins with her on the brink of enlightenment. She had achieved all the wisdom and virtue needed to ascend into nirvana, to leave the cycle of suffering behind forever. But as she stood at the threshold, ready to cross into eternal peace, she heard the cries of the world—the anguished voices of those still lost in their own Dark Forests.

In that moment, Quan Yin made an extraordinary choice. She turned back. She chose to stay in the realm of suffering, not out of obligation but out of boundless compassion. Her heart broke open for humanity, and in that breaking, it expanded to hold the pain of the world.

Quan Yin's Dark Forest is not her own but the collective shadows of humanity. She walks through it endlessly, offering her light to those who cannot yet see their way out. Her compassion is not a distant, ethereal concept; it is visceral, grounded in the understanding of what it means to suffer. She does not erase pain but holds it with tenderness, transforming it into a space for healing. The real Medicine Buddha.

For those moving through the Dark Forest, Quan Yin's story is a reminder that we are never alone. Her presence whispers that even in your most isolated moments, there is a thread of connection tying you to others who have walked this path. She teaches you that compassion—for yourself and others—is the key to emerging from the shadows with your heart intact.

There are universal patterns hidden in the forest.

The stories of Isis, Hecate, and Quan Yin reveal universal truths about the Dark Forest. Whether you walk into it driven by grief, choice, or compassion, the journey is one of transformation. The descent strips you of illusions, forcing you to face your raw, unfiltered self. The stillness teaches you to listen to the wisdom of your soul. And the ascent asks you to carry the lessons forward, forever changed by what you have endured.

These myths are not just ancient stories; they are mirrors of your own experience. They remind you that the darkness is not an ending but a beginning—a sacred initiation into your highest potential. And as you walk through the forest, you do so in the company of those who have come before you, their light guiding your way.

THE PATH FORWARD

Emerging from the Dark Forest is not the end of the journey; it is the beginning of something new. In the shadows, we unearth truths about ourselves—raw, unfiltered, and deeply authentic.

Yet, stepping back into the light after such an experience requires courage and intentionality. The wisdom gained in the forest must be integrated into your daily life, shaping how you live, love, and connect.

When you leave the forest, you are not the same. The world around you may look unchanged, but you carry within you the knowing of what you've endured. Integration is the process of weaving that knowing into the fabric of your everyday life. It is not an act of returning to what was but of building something completely new.

The lessons learned in the forest are seeds that you've planted within. They grow slowly, requiring patience and care. Maybe you learned to trust your intuition when all logic failed. Or you discovered the depth of your resilience and your strength. These are not fleeting lessons; they shape the way we navigate the world.

Rebuilding with wisdom often means honoring boundaries—energetic, emotional, and relational. The forest teaches you to say no to what no longer serves you and yes to what aligns with your truth. It invites you to create a life that reflects the authenticity you uncovered in the darkness. But this rebuilding is not without its challenges. The temptation to slip back into old patterns can be strong, especially when the comfort of familiarity calls. But the wisdom of the forest is a steady guide, reminding you that growth is a continuous, unfolding process.

The light discovered in the forest transforms the way you see yourself and the world around you.

Relationships take on new depth as we learn to connect from a place of authenticity rather than fear or obligation. Purpose becomes clearer, not because we suddenly know all the answers but because we are no longer afraid to ask the questions we need to take steps forward.

Living in alignment means walking through life with an openness to both the light and the dark. It's understanding that joy and sorrow are not opposites but companions, each enriching the other. The forest teaches us to embrace the full spectrum of our experience, knowing that even the painful moments hold value.

For some, this alignment manifests as a renewed sense of purpose. The forest strips away what is inessential, leaving only what truly matters. We may find ourselves drawn to new paths, careers, or creative pursuits that align with the deeper truth we discovered. For others, it is a shift in perspective—a softening, a willingness to approach life with curiosity and ease.

The transformation is not always dramatic. Sometimes it is as simple as choosing to greet each day with gratitude or holding space for someone else's pain without trying to fix it. But these small shifts ripple outward, creating a life that feels more vibrant and whole.

It is easy to think of the Dark Forest as something to escape, a chapter to close and leave behind. But true integration requires something deeper: gratitude.

The forest is a teacher. Stripping us down, not to destroy us but to reveal the strength, wisdom, and love we've always held within. The Dark Forest shouldn't be feared. It's a rite of passage that you must walk through to fully know your strength and purpose. It's within the darkness that you are stripped of illusion and taught the raw truth of who you are. The forest teaches us to embrace uncertainty, to trust our inner guidance, and to find our own way when the path ahead seems veiled in shadow. It's here that you find the wisdom that lights your way forward.

The journey through the forest isn't easy, and at times it feels as if there's no way out. But what you often forget is the darkness you want to escape is the very place you transform. The shadow is not your enemy—it is a companion guiding you to the most authentic version of yourself. Each step, each trial, each moment of confusion or fear brings you closer to your soul's truth. The darkness is where we grow, where we learn to hold both light and shadow with the energy of Grace.

Emerging from the forest is not an end but a beginning.

The wisdom we carry with us transforms the way we see the world, the way we love and the way we live. And this transformation isn't just for us—it's for everyone we encounter. As we walk forward, we are called to share the light we've uncovered with the world, to become the beacons of light and wisdom for others who may still find themselves in the shadows. This is the power of the journey: to not only heal and align ourselves but also empower others to walk the same path of discovery.

If you have walked through the forest, you have faced your fears, embraced your pain, and emerged stronger. You've gathered the pieces of your soul, and now it's time to shine. Your light, born from the darkest of places, has the power to illuminate the world around you. It's your story, your growth, your healing that will guide others through their own moments of darkness.

Embodying the lessons of the forest means living fully in alignment with the truth you have discovered. It means stepping into your purpose with courage, knowing that the challenges you've overcome were the very things that shaped you into the person you are meant to be. The forest has not broken you—it has forged you. And now, as you carry your light forward, you become a living testament to the power of transformation, to the power of embracing the duality of this world.

As you step out of the forest, know this: Every step has brought you closer to alignment with your soul's purpose. And though life will continue to present its challenges, you now walk with a steady well of inner knowing. You are no longer the person who entered the forest.

You are a light-bearer, walking with clarity, strength, and the courage to shine your light wherever you go.

Celebrate the courage you've had to face the unknown. Celebrate the wisdom you've gained through your trials. And remember—just as the forest was always a place of growth, so too is life. The forest may call you back from time to time, but when it does, you'll know you are never truly lost. You are simply returning to the sacred place where transformation continues.

Gratitude for the forest does not mean glorifying the pain or wishing it upon yourself again. It's honoring the gifts it brought—the resilience you didn't know you had, the clarity you couldn't have found any other way, and the compassion that deepened in the face of your own struggles.

This gratitude transforms how you view not just your own journey but the journeys of others. We begin to see the Dark Forest as a universal experience, one that connects us to every soul who's ever walked through its shadows. It emboldens your empathy, reminding you that we are never truly alone in the depths of our struggles.

Gratitude for the forest is a form of healing. It allows you to integrate the darkness into the wholeness of your being, a vital thread in the tapestry of your life. It teaches you to embrace the duality of existence—the light and the dark, the joy and the sorrow—as essential parts of the human experience.

The path forward is not a return to the life you knew but the start of something entirely new. We carry the forest within us—as a wellspring of wisdom and strength. It becomes a part of who we are, shaping the way we move through the world.

As you walk this new path, you do so with the understanding that the journey is ongoing. The light you carry illuminates the way as you continue to grow and evolve. And though the forest may call you back at times, you no longer fear its shadows. You know the darkness is not an end but a beginning—a sacred space of transformation—a place to *sit in the frequency of change.*

The Dark Forest is a gift, not because it's easy but because it's real. It reminds us of our capacity to endure, to heal, and to create.

And as you step forward, do so with gratitude—for the forest, for the light, and for the infinite possibilities that lie ahead.

You've got this. Keep going.

CHAPTER 4

FIND YOUR CENTER

Many people set out on a journey to discover their purpose and find their place in the world. But what we're really seeking is something much deeper: our center, the core of who we are. It's from this place that we can expand, create, and live in alignment with our highest good. The truth is, we never need to become anything other than who we already are. The answers we seek have always been within us. The challenge is quieting the noise around us, releasing the limiting beliefs that have kept us trapped in a framework that was never meant for us—a framework where our authentic self doesn't fit.

In being human, finding your center is not just a step; it's a required part of the path. This process demands that you break through the illusions you've inherited and uncover who you really are. Finding your center means stripping away the layers of learned behaviors, emotional baggage, and false narratives obscuring your gifts and authenticity. Part of the bargain of being you is unraveling the stories that have distorted your perception of who you really are.

Finding your center is not about becoming something new. It's about returning to the self that has always been there. Along the way, the process can be difficult, but every challenge is an opportunity to reclaim and uncover the parts of you that have been hidden. Earth isn't the easiest place—with its dense spectrum of emotions to navigate. It's normal to encounter resistance as we move toward our center.

The limiting beliefs we need to let go of built our current sense of identity. That's where the struggle lies: in dismantling the narratives that once defined who you are to reveal the truth of your authenticity at your core.

Obstacles will appear. This world was designed to challenge your sense of self and purpose—those challenges are all a part of the plan. The journey to your center is a path of peeling away the layers that no longer serve you, and as you do, you'll begin to see through the illusion, the perceptual matrix of foundational beliefs that aren't in alignment with your true self. The more you peel back, the more aligned you'll become with your authentic self.

The goal is to become the most aligned version of who you are.

One of the greatest shifts that comes from aligning with your center is understanding that your purpose here isn't focused on making everyone else happy. Your purpose is to embody your true self—to find your own joy, your own peace, and your own alignment. Source created you to be you! The more you step into your authenticity, the more you realize you're not meant to fit into someone else's mold. When you grow, you'll discover some of the people around you will no longer align with who you are, your morals and ideals, and your path. Please understand this is not a reflection of their wrongness; it's a reflection of your growth.

Part of the bargain of being you is releasing the attachment to others' opinions in favor of becoming your own compass. In releasing the need for external validation, you honor your authenticity. Finding your center is not a singular moment or static destination. It's a process that unfolds as you grow, as you change, as you peel back the layers of this world that have hid you from yourself.

This realm is inherently difficult, but it's time you lean in to the beauty of the difficulty. It's incredibly rewarding to find your center in the midst of struggle, in the midst of finding your strength. The challenge really does make all the obstacles feel worth it.

My greatest wish for you is that you get to look back and you see how far you've come. See how you've let go of the boundaries and restrictions that didn't belong to you and you step into the person you were always meant to be—a person that no matter how dire the circumstances, you leaned in to Faith and you found your center. Being human means accepting that while this realm may be difficult, it's also filled with immense opportunity for growth, transformation, and love.

You are a unique fractal of Source.

The opportunity to find your center is a gift and you are meant to enjoy the journey back to you.

THE MISSIONS WE CHOOSE

When we embark on a journey of personal growth, we start to ask ourselves things like: Why am I here? What's my life's purpose? How did I end up where I ended up? Why is my life like this? These questions are more than just intrusive thoughts—they're the echoes of your soul speaking to the agreements we made before we entered into this life.

Our lives are not a random collection of events but carefully chosen experiences unfolding according to the missions we chose before we arrived, before we were born into these bodies.

We live a fated life intertwined with free will.

Accepting fated events as an integral part of life makes reaching your higher self easier. Through being human, we agreed to certain terms and conditions. You chose to be here. Your soul signed up for the adventures, comfortable or not, that you experience when you volunteered to come here.

We chose the very life we're in, and while some of these experiences can be difficult, your soul understood the benefit they offer. The themes of your life and the lessons you learn through them provide massive growth for the soul, and the collective as a whole.

You made a bargain to be here, and it's time to learn what exactly you signed up for.

To unravel your missions, we have to look at the patterns, themes, and lessons that have repeatedly surfaced through your life. Recurring themes act as a map for your journey—pointing you toward the lessons you are meant to learn in this lifetime to reach your potential. The patterns show you where you made agreements for growth.

Your life is woven like a tapestry, and every thread—every challenge, every victory—forms a pattern that reveals your path. The challenges we face are not arbitrary. They are invitations to complete your soul's mission. The obstacles you encounter serve as the tests you overcome to fulfill your growth.

Hindsight is a beautiful thing. Reflecting will allow you to see the patterns—the grand design you're a part of.

A theme many face is the *challenge of learning self-love and self-worth.* This mission presents itself in difficult relationships, limiting beliefs, and societal pressures that leave you feeling like you're not enough. When navigating this path, you can easily find yourself seeking validation from external sources, chasing acceptance, and readily falling into patterns of highly critical self-talk. The mission you are asked to fulfill is one of reclaiming your inherent worth—not from the outside world—but by turning inward and connecting with the love you can generate from within. Life presents opportunities to break free from the cycles of people-pleasing, perfectionism, and self-sabotage you learn through. It's a process of healing the wounds of rejection, abandonment, and betrayal that lead you to believe you were unworthy of love. If these themes feel familiar, your worth comes from within before it will reflect back from the outside world. Transform through this theme and the lessons it provides, and you'll feel and experience the love you're looking for.

Learning to *overcome fear and embrace courage with Faith* is another biggie in the life themes department. Fear can manifest in countless ways—fear of failure, fear of rejections, fear of change, and even fear of success. Transforming through this theme will result in countless experiences challenging your comfort zone—forcing you into the shadow to shed light on the things you fear. You'll find yourself holding back, avoiding risks, and retreating to your comfort zone, only to be faced with circumstances that ask you to rise above fear once more. It's part of the mission to realize fear isn't a real obstacle but a compass, guiding you back to the areas you need to heal. Faith is always present when fear presents itself. She'll ask you to build resilience and belief in your capabilities as you move through fear. Fear is a limiting force—while Faith is limitless. The process of moving through and away from fear requires deep inner work. Reprogramming old beliefs and embodying the willingness to fail as many times as needed is required. With each step taken, your courage and confidence grows—expanding the possibility of reaching your potential. Bold choices, new adventures, and leaning in to the unknown is part of the mission for your highest potential. Embrace the force of Faith—she's relentless when conquering fear.

One of the most challenging themes is *healing from grief and loss.* Navigating this path results in significant losses—whether it be the passing of loved ones, relationships ending, or the loss of your life path and identity—grief hurts. It brings with it an intense range of emotions, from deep sorrow and anger to confusion and loneliness. The theme of grief is about learning to process the emotions in a way that honors your experience—without allowing the pain to close you off from future loving and joyful experiences.

Honoring this life theme means embracing the impermanence of life and understanding that while loss is inevitable, it serves a greater purpose in our evolution. Healing from grief isn't about moving on or forgetting; it's about integrating the experience in a way that allows the heart to remain open. It takes courage to confront the pain loss creates. Sitting with it and ultimately finding peace in the void is one of life's hardest lessons. Healing through grief allows you to develop an appreciation for life's fleeting moments—finding meaning that transcends our physical experience.

Learning to navigate your life themes, with their unique challenges, can cause a need for more than just one life. Reincarnation is often misunderstood as a punishment or failure to get it right the first time. The truth is, reincarnation is a gift—a means of allowing the soul to return and continue the growth we have left to complete. Some of the hardest lessons, where we transform dense emotions like guilt and shame, can require more than one lifetime to clear. If you're a soul that feels like you're burning through generations of pain and trauma, you're more advanced than you realize. With each incarnation, you gain new insights, new strength, and the ability to transform the seemingly impossible experiences into divine light and wisdom.

The timing in which you accomplish these missions doesn't follow that of your analytical mind. The soul operates on a scale more expansive than our understanding of time—one that doesn't adhere to the restrictions of the illusion of linear time. It's the mind that believes you should have learned your lessons sooner, that you should have seen the truth of situations before you did. Your higher self knows better—it knows that everything happens in divine timing. The soul, the higher self, doesn't need to rush. Every lesson is integrated precisely when it's meant to be, not a moment sooner.

Evolving and growing spirituality requires the acceptance of divine timing.

Phrases like "I wish I had known sooner" or "If only I had seen it earlier" are born from the mind's desire for control and certainty. But the higher self, rooted in infinite wisdom, knows that if we had learned something earlier, we wouldn't have evolved in the time that was necessary for our highest path. Our lives are divinely orchestrated as a vast web of interconnected events.

Source and our higher selves are not bound by the earthly concepts of time.

Fully embracing being led by your higher self requires the acceptance of divine timing—integrating that understanding is part of the mission.

THE SOULS WE MEET

Through the missions we choose and the life themes we play out, we inevitably encounter other souls along the way. Some will uplift you, providing clarity and light on your journey, while others will challenge you, serving as your catalysts for growth. Every soul you meet plays a role in your evolution. Whether they are a source of joy or resistance, their presence in your life is purposeful. In life there will be heroes and there will be villains—which one is which is determined by the perspective you see.

In this complex web of existence, no meeting is by chance. The people we encounter—whether for a moment or a lifetime—are part of the mission being carried out. Life here is not about being right or wrong. Things are not black and white, light and dark. It's a combination—we learn by experiencing the gray. Elevating your experience isn't about eliminating dense experiences altogether; it's about settling into your authentic frequency and experiencing every moment with as much presence as you can . . . good, bad, and somewhere in between.

Every soul has a unique perspective—with their own life to live.

As we move through life, we realize how interconnected we all are. The missions we choose, while deeply personal, have a profound impact on the collective. Each bit of growth, every lesson learned, moves a wave of energy out into the world, raising the vibration and elevating consciousness on Earth. While you may feel isolated at times, you are a fractal of Source, and everything around you and inside you is connected.

This is why self-love, healing, and personal transformation are not selfish acts. They're necessary for the collective growth of humanity. When you heal yourself—overcoming the density of guilt, shame, and fear—you contribute to healing the entire collective. We are all participating in a grand evolutionary process, each playing our part—whether we're aware of it or not.

The people who challenge you the most, acting as resistance to your progress, provide most of your opportunities for growth. These souls, seemingly unaware of the resistance they create, give you the chance to practice—nonjudgment and unconditional love. We play out our missions, day by day, moment by moment. Some of us wake up and have an awareness of our connectedness—some stay asleep their entire lives. Some take lifetimes to wake up and some never do. These souls offer you the opportunity to see the difference between your veiled and unveiled experience. They offer the necessary contrast in our lives, and they give us an opportunity to find the light through the darkness.

Honor the contrast; it's part of why we are all here.

When we look at nature, we see diversity everywhere—every species, every ecosystem, shows us the harmony that comes from many different life forms working together. The same is true for us. We excel at different things. We find joy in different activities, occupations, and hobbies.

We need to celebrate where we fit. Our journeys are unique. Allowing yourself to fit in where your intuition leads you, where your joy is found, allows you to live your intended experience. It's an experience that is authentic to you.

The missions you choose are not without difficulty. You will face pain and joy, sorrow and bliss. But life isn't about having an all-or-nothing experience. Life will always be a blend of beautiful contrast that helps you find your center. Your soul grows through this balance—you learn to love through the resistance.

Embrace your mission with an open heart.

Learn to love who you are. Learn to be as kind to yourself as you are to others. Learn to express yourself while embracing your authenticity.

Learn to follow your joy.

Explore the themes of your life. Sometimes the best way to figure out who you are is to realize who you are not.

THE ENERGY WE TRANSMUTE

Change is woven into the fabric of our very existence. At the heart of the human experience lies the potential for massive transformation—not just in our physical form but in our consciousness, our emotional state, how we think, and our energy. We have the capability for continual change and growth—bearing witness to many death and rebirth cycles within a single lifetime on Earth. All the change in your life is an epic unfolding of the authentic self.

And in this unfolding, we learn to be grateful for every moment we've lived—even the painful and difficult ones. Because when we move through dense emotions—like fear, grief, guilt, shame, and anger—finding peace and gratitude instead, we participate in the process of alchemy. We transmute energy by shifting our emotional state. Emotions are energy in motion, after all, carrying vibrational frequencies that reflect where we are in our journey. By transmuting these energies, we create the environment needed for more aligned versions of ourselves.

Earth is a unique place to learn this process. The density of the planet, with all its hardships and contrasting experiences, provides the perfect environment to learn how to move and transform energy. Earth provides a depth of experience you cannot get anywhere else, and it's through the challenging environment that you master your abilities. Every bit of density turned into light affects the collective—every bit you heal changes the sum of the vibration of the whole.

Ascension is not an abstract concept; it's the natural result of emotional and energetic healing. As you transmute energy through healing, you raise your individual and collective vibration—deepening your connection to a greater understanding of existence. This process is what gives you access to higher states of compassion and love. You have the ability to take pain and suffering and turn it into something beautiful—and it's part of your mission to do so. Your healing becomes the key that unlocks the doorway into other realms of understanding.

As you embody higher frequencies, you act as beacons of possibility for those around you, showing them that they too can transform. But we can only guide others as far as we have journeyed ourselves. The level with which we have healed is the upper limit where we can be of service to others.

It's in healing ourselves that we show others what is possible.

When you fall into the trap of comparing your journey to others, you stall your growth. The speed of your healing, the depth of your challenges, and the nature of your lessons are all perfectly aligned with your soul's plan. And while it may be easy to dismiss your struggles when you measure them against someone else, the truth is every experience holds meaning and purpose. Some came here to transmute generational trauma—clearing the dense energies passed down through their genetic line. Others are here to work through personal karma, healing the wounds they've carried through lifetimes.

Regardless of what you're working on, the process is powerful, and the impact of your healing moves energy out into the collective consciousness.

The missions we choose can be all-consuming, and they can also be much more subtle. Embrace the journey you're on, no matter how it unfolds. Every challenge faced, every emotion you transmute, every layer of healing you accomplish has a purpose.

The fact that you're here shows how valued you are—remember that.

Your authenticity is your greatest gift. You were born for this.

We rise through the remembering—through our bargain with Faith, accessing our truth, feeling the pain of being alive, and being present through all of it. But awakening alone isn't enough. Once you've cracked yourself open and seen what's real, you have to learn how to *live* life from that place. *That's where the work begins again.* The next phase of the journey asks something different from you. It asks you to regulate—to bring safety to your nervous system, stillness to your mind, and steadiness to the soul that's learning how to stay awake in a world still fast asleep.

Let's step into the next part of the path, where you'll learn how to hold all that you've awakened to—without burning out, breaking down, or shutting off.

It's time to learn how to *Regulate.*

You've got this. Keep going.

PART II

Regulate

Change is inevitable–it's the only constant in this world. Knowing this gives us the opportunity to make the process of change easier on ourselves–giving us one of the keys to unlocking our true potential. There will be components of our physical and mental experience that when our analytical mind understands them in advance, we're able to navigate changes in life with Grace, instead of resistance. *I think we would all agree that ease is something we could use more of.* We stop fighting against ourselves. We learn to reduce the resistance we encounter.

When you understand the anatomy of change, everything becomes easier.

Change in and of itself isn't what causes you pain. It's the resistance to change that hurts. The more resistance you create, the more painful your life transitions will be. Once we understand the anatomy of change, we stop building resistance. We lean in to the impermanence of life and find our alignment through our changing experiences. Change is not something to be feared—it's a powerful force connecting you to your most beautiful experiences. Let's learn to embrace it.

There are four essential life systems involved in the anatomy of change—energetic, mental, emotional, and physical.

These systems are connected and impact each other every step of the way. When you understand how these systems work and impact each other, you unlock more empowered versions of yourself through regulating every area of who you are.

The process of healing is a process of trial and error. You figure out how everything works as you move along. You stumble, learn, and adjust. *But what if you knew the foundational pillars ahead of time?* You'd surely move along your path a lot swifter, with more ease and understanding.

You'd be a lot more comfortable accepting Grace if you understood what you've agreed to navigate through in advance.

Change is so difficult because we don't understand it. It's unpredictable. Our analytical mind craves understanding, and when it doesn't get it, it causes us to feel a wide range of emotions, fear, and heavy resistance. But what if we simply understood the anatomy of change up front? The major resistance we face and feel when it comes to change would dissolve. *Understanding the process makes a difference.* It provides an opportunity to align with the analytical mind instead of fighting against it. Learning the interconnected systems of change and how to regulate them is part of being human. It's part of understanding who you are as a soul experiencing life through the human experience and a human body.

It's time to remove the obstacles and open yourself up to what's possible—the very real, unlimited nature of who you are. You have the ability to reach your authentic self.

You are worthy of understanding the operating manual for this life.

Understanding the anatomy of change and what it takes to *Regulate* each system will impact every area of your life. You'll gain the confidence to move through transitional times with ease. Understanding, no matter how things look in the moment, the future is beautiful.

When you know why you feel the way you feel, everything becomes a lot easier.

You've got this. Keep going.

CHAPTER 5

THE ENERGETIC BODY

We have to pay close attention to our energetic body—the part of you that you can't always see but you can absolutely feel.

The energetic body is connected to everything we experience, and because of that, it's not something we heal in isolation. It's affected by all aspects of who we are—the things we've healed and the lessons we've learned or still have yet to figure out. Your energetic body will change with how closely your alignment is with your authentic self.

The energetic body is your soul's vibrational resonance here on Earth, and it's constantly interacting with everything around you. It's the unspoken introduction you make when you meet others, the magnet that draws in your manifestations, and it's the way you send signals out into the world in your attempts to connect with your soul family. We are able to impact the world and the world impacts us through our energetic body. The energetic body is an essential part of you even though you don't see it, and it's not something we're readily taught about . . . yet.

The truth is, the energetic body affects your mental, emotional, and physical health. *How many times have you felt physically off or experienced some sort of health problem without a clear cause?* It's because it's all connected. We have to look at ALL of the systems of life. The cause isn't always located where the symptom is.

When you change something in your energy, you influence the other life systems—and the reverse is true too. Altering your physical body will shift your energy. Altering your emotional state will shift your energy. Altering your mental state will shift your energy. And vice versa. All of it is working together to create your experience of the reality you live in.

And while the energetic body was once considered some spiritual woo-woo thing, science is catching up to what mystics have known for ages. Every day we're finding new ways to measure energetic fields and quantum entanglement and exploring how the web of consciousness impacts our health and well-being. We now have tools that can show us the shifts in a person's energy centers as they heal and come into alignment with their authentic selves through practices like meditation. Energy centers align and grow as a direct result of healing work.

You want to think of your energetic body like your physical body. Your overall energetic field is like the physical body as a whole, energy centers are like organs, and your energy flow moves through channels like your veins and nerves that keep everything communicating and flowing. Many mystical traditions and practices reference these systems by various names—what I want you to understand is the mechanics of the energetic body system because regardless of the terms we use to describe it, how everything works is the same.

In the future, it's likely we'll develop a universal language for the energetic system, just as we have for the heart and lungs. For now, what matters most is that you understand the power you hold in your energy.

When you learn to operate the energetic body in harmony with your other life systems, you find alignment with your highest, most authentic self.

It's time to unlock new levels of consciousness, elevate your well-being, and create an aligned and fulfilling experience for your life.

ENERGY HYGIENE

In the same way we tend to our physical body for health and wellness, we also need to tend to our personal energy field. Energy hygiene is an essential and often overlooked piece of our well-being.

Energetic hygiene is just as vital as brushing your teeth, taking a shower, eating healthy food, and exercising your body. When you neglect your physical hygiene, odors linger, infections can occur, and your overall health declines. The same thing happens with energetic hygiene. The consequences are just more subtle and can be confused with other body systems. When your energy field isn't properly taken care of, it can become clogged and harshly impacted by external influences. Over time, this can lead to fatigue, mental fog, an inability to regulate emotions, and even physical pain and discomfort.

When you make energetic hygiene part of your daily routine, it allows you to move through the world in a way where you are able to understand which energy is yours and which energy is from the world around you. When we maintain our energetic fields, we navigate life with more ease, walk with Grace, and find fulfilling our purpose to be enjoyable. Cleansing your energetic body will allow you to not only maintain a higher vibration but also expand your capacity for higher vibrational experiences filled with abundance and joy.

So, what is energetic hygiene?

At its core, energetic hygiene is the practice of regularly cleansing, maintaining, and protecting your energy field. It's about recognizing the different energetic inputs you encounter every day and understanding the influence they have on your emotional, mental, and physical body systems. Once you become aware of how energy works, you can consciously take part in practices that help you stay in your alignment, free from as much resistance as possible.

Developing an energetic hygiene practice empowers you to create the reality you desire. Manifesting your highest potential requires that you are mindful of what you allow into your personal energy field. Being selective of the inputs you expose yourself to is an act of self-love, respect, and care. The choices we make are a direct reflection of the alignment we reside in. Choose wisely.

ENERGETIC INPUTS

Energy is everywhere. Every interaction, every conversation, every environment you enter—everything has its own frequency, and all of it can have an impact on you, if you let it. Some energetic inputs will uplift us, filling us with light, positivity, and inspiration. Others can weigh us down, leaving us drained, anxious, and irritable. The key to understanding energy is learning to discern the difference. Once you do, you can take the necessary steps to manage your energetic inputs as effectively as you can.

Let's start with the people in your life. *Every person you come in contact with affects your energy in some way.* Think about the people closest to you, that you spend the most time with—friends, family, co-workers, and so on. Over time, their energy intertwines with yours. The more time you spend with someone, the more tangled your energy is with theirs. We've all experienced being around someone who makes us laugh and elevates our energy and the opposite with those who leave us feeling exhausted and drained. These interactions are not just an emotional reaction to different people . . . they're energetic.

If you're not mindful of your energy hygiene, you can absorb the dense, lower-vibrational energy of those who operate from a place of doom and gloom. Over time this takes a toll on your energy field, making it harder to maintain a higher vibrational state, slowing your trajectory toward your manifestations. On the other hand, surrounding yourself with people who reflect the energy you want to embody—people who are supportive, are loving, and see the silver linings—naturally helps you elevate your frequency.

Like draws to like, so if you're surrounded by people carrying messages of doom and gloom it's important to check in with yourself before pointing any fingers. *How are you speaking to yourself and others? Mostly positive or mostly negative?* We are responsible for the vibes just as much as anyone else and perfection is not the goal. Awareness and management is.

This is where boundaries come into play. Boundaries are not just about protecting yourself from harm; they preserve your energy. Healthy boundaries allow you to engage with other people on your own terms, limiting the influence of those who drain you while opening the door to deeper connections with those who uplift you.

Setting boundaries is one of the most powerful practices of energetic hygiene.

It allows you to navigate the quality of energy you interact with every day.

Setting boundaries will be difficult at times. Some people, especially those who have been in your life and have had unlimited access to your energy, may resist and push back when you start limiting their access to your energy. The discomfort initially is part of the process. As you move toward your higher self and access your true frequency, not everyone will come with you. It takes courage to let go of relationships that no longer serve you, but in doing so, you create the space for those who are aligned with your highest path.

Every relationship will be different. Some will see the boundaries as an attack against them, while others will see boundaries as a mirror allowing for their own self-improvement and growth. It's our job to honor our own healing journey while giving the people around us the space to be whomever they are destined to be. Sometimes this results in improved relationships, and sometimes it means we let people go on their journey without us. Have the courage to allow relationships to end when they need to.

Sexual intimacy in relationships is a powerful form of an energetic exchange. When you engage in these intimate acts, you open your energy field, creating energetic cords with your partner. These energetic entanglements can linger long after the physical act, impacting your emotional and mental state into the foreseeable future. The more intimate partners you have, the more complicated your energetic web becomes. This is why so many who are walking the path of healing and awakening are becoming highly selective with whom they share their sexual energy with.

Sexual energy is life force energy. Whichever partner is in the higher vibrational state will inadvertently take on some of the lower-vibrational energies of the other person in an attempt to transmute them. For most people, this process is completed without an awareness of the energy exchange, and it can have a lasting emotional and energetic impact on the person absorbing these energies. Being mindful who you exchange this energy with can protect you from taking on lower-vibrational energies and ensure that the emotional and energetic work you do is your own until you consciously choose otherwise.

When considering energetic inputs, we also have to be mindful of the collective energy around us. Large gatherings, such as concerts, protests, sporting events, and even crowded shopping centers can leave you feeling depleted and overwhelmed. They can also make you feel uplifted, excited, and hopeful. It depends on the collective energy of the group. As you expand your understanding of energy, you'll become more aware of how certain settings make you feel.

The neighborhoods we live in, the places we work, the stores we shop, the restaurants we dine in, and the public transportation we use can uplift us or drain us. It's part of the bargain of being you to learn how you are affected and lean in to what lifts you up versus what pulls you down.

Then there's the media we consume. We are constantly bombarded with information—news, social media, television, and advertising—all of which have their own frequency and vibration. What we pay attention to will either help us break through our limiting beliefs or reinforce them. When you pay attention to media that promotes fear, anger, and division, you lower your vibration. On the other hand, when you surround yourself with content that inspires, uplifts, and brings a sense of peace, you naturally rise. The more aware you are of the energy you consume through media, the more you are able to navigate and improve your own energetic state.

Being aware of the comings and goings of the world and maintaining your predominant focus on the silver lining is a delicate balance.

Focus on the good. It grows when you do.

DEVELOPING A DAILY PRACTICE

Energetic hygiene isn't a onetime event—it's a daily practice. Just as you wouldn't skip brushing your teeth or showering for days on end, you need the same pull to take care of your energetic field. Make energy hygiene practices a regular part of your routine, something you do instinctively to maintain your health, happiness, and clarity.

The first step is leaning in to the boundaries you need with the inputs in your life. This might mean limiting time with certain people, removing yourself from negative environments, and turning off the news when it becomes overwhelming. Setting boundaries isn't about cutting yourself off from the world—it's about consciously choosing where you direct your energy. Hours of doomscrolling isn't helpful, but taking a couple of minutes to consume content that actually feels relaxing and inspiring should be enjoyed. Don't be afraid to start small with your boundaries and increase them over time as you gain confidence. As you heal and grow, you'll adjust your boundaries with the energetic inputs in your life, making it easier for what needs to stay and what needs to leave. Start wherever you are. This isn't about being perfect. It's about making progress.

Boundaries are the rules of engagement with which we engage with the world.

They show the world how you really feel about yourself, regardless of what you say. And as you move through the process of healing, you gain clarity, allowing you to see where you shortchanged yourself with a lack of healthy boundaries. You begin to see where you undervalued who you are, and you make the necessary adjustments. Focus on holding one new boundary. Every one after is easier than the first.

Next step is cleansing. Daily cleansing practices are essential for removing any energetic "gunk" you pick up throughout the day. One of the simplest, yet most powerful, ways to cleanse your energy field is through intention setting.

First thing in the morning, take a few moments to center yourself, connect with your breath, and set an intention for how you want to feel and show up in the world for the day. In doing this, you take the lead of your energy before anything else has had a chance to influence it.

Including mindfulness into your daily routine can also help you stay attuned to your energy throughout the day. Pay attention to how different situations, people, and environments make you feel. If you notice your energy taking a turn for the worse, take a moment to breathe deeply and tune in to yourself. The 7-7-7-7 breathing is my go-to and is what I recommend.

> Breathe in for seven counts, hold for seven, exhale for seven, and hold for seven more. Repeat this cycle until you feel your energy return.

You can always focus on your breath in stressful moments. Breath is quiet and personal. Focusing on your breath shifts your energy in a manner that is rarely noticed by those around you. When you feel anxiety build in your body, that's an indication you need to focus on your breath. In these moments, the nervous system is being activated as the physical system is connected to the energetic. Learn to use your breath when navigating the world, and your energy will become clearer with each opportunity you practice.

Physical movement is another powerful way to cleanse your energy field. Whether you choose yoga, dancing, or going for a walk, movement helps release energy. Taking a few minutes to move will help you release the energy of the day and will get you moving when you feel energetically stuck.

Many people, myself included, find water rituals like taking a shower can cleanse the energetic field.

> As you stand under the water, visualize any dense or sticky energy being washed away. Repeat the visualization until you feel lighter and more yourself. If you feel like you need an extra boost of cleansing on difficult days, use your hands to physically wipe off the energy as the water flows.

Many people who become sensitive and aware of their energetics will shift their showers from the mornings to the evenings because that allows them to combine the physical practice of cleansing off the dirt of the world with the energetic. This becomes a nightly ritual for them, allowing them to disengage from the world's energy before entering their bedrooms for the night.

If you need a practice that is more readily available, an energetic screening is an excellent tool to remove unwanted energy.

Find a quiet place, close your eyes, and imagine a screen of light slowly moving down your body from the top of your head down to your toes, collecting any dense, heavy energy. As the screen moves, see yourself sending the collected energy into the earth's core to be transmuted. The earth recycles these energies into beautiful, life-giving environments. This simple visualization can be done in just a few minutes and is highly effective at clearing your energy field.

If the day was particularly dense or if it feels like a buildup of energy is still present, it may be helpful to use several screens capable of capturing smaller and smaller particles of energy. This practice allows us to become lighter and brighter with each screen we use.

Energetic hygiene is not just a feel-good practice—it directly impacts your physical, emotional, and spiritual well-being. Simple practices make a huge difference. Incorporating energetic hygiene practices into your daily routine will reduce stress, improve sleep, and improve your physical self as well as your energetic health. They will also align you with higher vibrational experiences, bringing more joy, abundance, and love into your life.

Move with intention. Be persistent. And practice patience.

You've got this. Keep going.

CHAPTER 6

THE MENTAL BODY

The mental body is one of the most challenging aspects to navigate. It's where your analytical mind lives—the thing in control of the operating software of the body we're moving around in.

The analytical mind really enjoys control. It craves predictability and seeks to create order in the world by categorizing everything into logical steps and patterns. The thing is, when we begin to tap into our intuition, we run into a problem. Intuition doesn't run on logic. Intuition is driven by the higher self, a knowing that flies above the rigid structure of "rational" thought.

This is where a lot of us get stuck. The mental body operates like a computer program, functioning in absolutes—it's all or nothing, black or white, right or wrong. This way of thinking limits our ability to reach our potential and creates a lot of the resistance we encounter with change. Especially if the change requires us to step into unknown territory. This is why, when you work on healing the mental body, you have to take steps to bypass the analytical mind and rewire the foundation of your beliefs, since that is what the mind is making assumptions from.

Healing the mental body is about reshaping the framing of your beliefs so that they support the life you truly desire and deserve. By removing limiting beliefs and installing the ones you want, you give your analytical mind the ability to operate in alignment with your higher self, reducing your resistance to change.

BELIEFS AND RESTRICTIVE THINKING

Beliefs are the main structure of your mental body. They shape the way you navigate the world, setting the stage for what you believe is possible, what you believe you are worthy of and how you think the world will respond to you.

Our thoughts can limit us or elevate us and what we believe about ourselves and our capabilities, especially in the beginning, stems from a belief structure that isn't our own. Our belief structure is put into place while we are very young. Our mind starts out as a blank slate, and by age eight we end up with a foundational structure for what we believe. The decisions we make about the world and our understanding of self all come from the belief structure set in place during our earliest stages of life.

Your brain is designed to absorb the environment around you when you're young. You take in every statement, every directive, every facial expression, the tone that's used when adults are speaking. What the brain takes in becomes the framework for your understanding of the world. We do this naturally, absorbing everything around us so that our brain can set the parameters required to alert you if you are safe or unsafe. The initial programming of your brain is a survival system—it's designed to help you recognize threats, get the nourishment you need for your body and keep you safe.

Through this process, we take in much more than we realize, including beliefs and patterns that may not ultimately serve us.

Restrictive thinking impacts every area of your life, confining not only you but also the world around you and the ones you love into limited possibilities. When you restrict what you believe is possible, you limit the actions you're willing to take, ultimately leading you to a life that isn't in alignment with your true self.

Restrictive thinking can be linked back to limiting beliefs embedded in the framework of the mind.

These beliefs manifest as negative thought patterns—about yourself, others, and the world—that hold you back from realizing your full potential. They come from your childhood programming, experiences, and societal conditioning, creating a self-fulfilling prophecy that reinforces unhealthy and limiting behaviors.

Some examples of common limiting beliefs are: I'm not good enough, I don't deserve success, I'm too old/young, I'm not smart enough, I don't have enough time/money/resources, I'm not attractive enough. The list goes on and on.

To start dismantling these beliefs, you have to take an inventory. *Start by writing down every limiting thought you believe to be true.* This exercise is simple and powerful—allow yourself to recognize that anywhere a limit exists, that limit can be removed. Some limiting beliefs will be obvious to you. Others may remain hidden until you're ready to tackle the task of reprogramming them. Let go of the idea that every limiting belief you have needs to be changed immediately.

Healing the mental body of negative thought patterns takes time. Some beliefs cannot be changed until we heal others. Some will be easy, and some will not. The mental body is a complex system. There's lots of nooks and crannies for these thoughts to hide in.

Beliefs create neural networks in the mind, hardwiring themselves into your brain and your body.

It can take multiple attempts at reprogramming before you find all the connections attached to a seemingly simple thought. *These connections influence your career, limiting the type of work you pursue and the boundaries you set for work-life balance.* They also shape your beliefs in your ability to advance and be compensated fairly for your efforts.

They affect relationships. They can create communication barriers and a lack of trust and stir up fears of rejection. These beliefs cause a lack of intimacy, too little or too many boundaries, and an inability to sense aligned choices regarding romantic partners and friends. They can lead to a whole host of self-sabotaging behaviors, limiting happiness, joy, and fulfillment in relationships.

Negative thought patterns can also have a major impact on your health. They have the ability to create a chronic state of stress in the body. Heart disease, diabetes, autoimmune disease, high blood pressure, anxiety, depression, and cancer are all linked with chronic stress. Restrictive beliefs can also block your ability to make beneficial changes to your health. When you feel unworthy, you block your well-being. It's easy to make poor choices when there isn't a belief that you deserve or could stick to the change you are attempting.

Unraveling these beliefs is a gradual process—a process that requires awareness, patience, and being relentless in your practice.

Start with awareness, taking note of every limiting thought. Where do you say *I can't* instead of *I can*?

Paying attention to your thoughts and how you speak about yourself in front of others is an exercise in awareness. How often are you limiting or speaking negatively of yourself?

Are you putting yourself down in front of other people to make them feel more comfortable? Coping mechanisms like self-deprecating humor end up being not so funny when we realize everything we say contributes to the reality we manifest.

Are you able to accept compliments without making a counter-comment? Or do you immediately put yourself down when complimented?

Awareness isn't about judgment. Most limiting beliefs are absorbed from your environment, but once you become conscious of them, they're your responsibility to change. Every transformed thought elevates not only your individual vibration but also that of the collective consciousness. As you heal, you raise the capacity for future generations to experience higher states of being.

Have the courage to face your limiting beliefs.

You're making the world a better place when you do.

Patience is required for this process to be successful.

Changing limiting beliefs happens over time. It's not a onetime fix at all. You start by accessing the most obvious of your limiting beliefs, and from there it becomes a scavenger hunt through the mind, finding all the places and spaces where the belief has a neural network attached. Some beliefs are deeply wired, while others are more surface level. No two beliefs have the same structure in the mind.

When patience becomes thin, it's important to remember how long these beliefs have been held. Beliefs from decades past are going to take more time to remove. Their neural networks are more ingrained in the mind. Altering your life trajectory from one of limitations and expectations to one of authentic expression and joy is like changing the direction of a cargo ship in port. The ship can take a large distance to simply slow to a stop. Then there is the time spent unloading all the cargo that is no longer making the journey with the ship. The ship has to gather its new cargo, sometimes over multiple ports, and then it takes massive effort to turn around and gain momentum going in a different direction again.

This journey often requires multiple destinations to off-load beliefs while picking up new ones along the way. Every step offers new learning opportunities to expand your understanding of yourself and Source. Every moment we exist is truly a gift—and shifting your perspective into gratitude for the journey, bumps and bruises included, allows you to experience what a beautiful adventure life is.

Make friends with the force of Faith on this journey.

Reprogramming your beliefs and initiating change can be uncomfortable and exhausting. There will be moments when you feel like giving up, but these are mere tests of your ability to walk the path with Faith. Faith is a beautiful force that sees the potential you have within you. Faith sees your beautiful future. Dig deep into your power. You can and will break through your perceived barriers when you do.

It's uncomfortable to transform before the new reality settles in. Hold onto the force of Faith.

She has her hand out—allow yourself to be led.

Reprogramming your beliefs opens pathways of growth, fulfillment, creativity, and confidence in your abilities. It's impossible for you to know how powerful you can be in the transformation process until you overcome the negative places and spaces you once believed were your fate.

They are not your fate.

REPROGRAMMING BELIEFS

So, how do you reprogram your beliefs? First, you need to develop an awareness of your beliefs. You need to observe them. You need to know how they are operating, what areas of your life they are impacting, and how often you hear the belief repeated.

For starters, you need to write down what you believe. You need to know what you believe about yourself and the world around you. Most of us don't even realize what we believe and what our limiting beliefs are until we take the time to focus on them. When we allow ourselves the opportunity to really look at the beliefs we've been living by, we gain the insight we need to see our beliefs for what they are, helpful or hurtful. Once you see what your beliefs are and how they are categorized, you can start to determine which ones you should keep and which ones you need to work on reprogramming.

Sometimes we need to take additional steps, particularly with negative beliefs, to gather the evidence we have that the belief is true. It's important to write down any experiences you've had that support or deny your negative beliefs. When you go through evidence gathering, you'll find the foundations for your beliefs are not rooted in truth. The process shows you what you should let go of, where you need to heal, and where you genuinely need heart-to-heart conversations about becoming a more evolved version of yourself. Compile the evidence for your beliefs. Write the evidence down and have the courage to examine it.

Once you know what your beliefs are, which ones are helpful and which ones you need to change, it's time to reframe the beliefs you are reprogramming. Write down the beliefs you would like to change. Then write the positive belief you are reprogramming the negative one with. Go belief by belief. Example: "I'm not smart enough." becomes "I'm always learning and growing. I have the skills and knowledge I need to succeed in every moment."

Once all your limiting beliefs have been reframed, honor the work you've done. Take the pages with the limiting beliefs and burn them, safely. This process aids in a powerful energetic release as you focus on the new positive beliefs instead. The practice of burning old beliefs alchemizes the energy cord tied between you and them. The feelings you feel, the conversations you have with your Creator and guides in this moment don't need to be preplanned. Feel your way through your ceremonial removal, saying what feels right from your heart, and when they've all been burned, hold to the intention that you've let them go.

Once the beliefs have been reframed and the energy cords between you and the old beliefs have been severed, it's time for patience and persistence to come into play. The game of repetition begins. *New beliefs need to be repeated and reinforced continuously.* That's how the limiting beliefs became incorporated in your neural networks to begin with. The process of installing their opposite is the same.

Use the following steps until the new beliefs have been installed.

- **Write them:** The act of writing activates neural networks in your brain. This solidifies the new neural pathway much sooner than speaking, reading, or internal self-talk will. Write them in a journal every day. Commit to it and watch it work.
- **Speak them:** Your internal and external dialogue shapes your reality. Act as if your new beliefs are true—because they are. Catch yourself when old patterns of thought or speech arise. Progress, not perfection, is the goal. If you keep speaking in limiting ways, you can't expect to manifest

an unlimited future. Push through the discomfort, and repeatedly return to the new beliefs you are installing. Be relentless in believing in your transformation–it's already happening.

- **See them:** Meditation is an invaluable tool for integrating new beliefs. It allows you to tap into an expanded awareness, where you can visualize and *feel* yourself living as your unlimited self. Meditation is where you connect with your higher self and receive guidance from your spiritual team. Deeper meditations, like The Awakening Series I offer, will help you access the brain's structural programming and facilitate lasting change. Use this tool to see the version of yourself that you want to manifest and create in the physical realm.
- **Commit to the process.**

Set these steps on repeat until your new beliefs take root. *Be patient* with yourself—long-standing thought patterns take time and effort to change. The struggle of reprogramming is part of the process. When you feel weighed down by limiting beliefs, remember that you are not just learning to think differently—you're transforming into a more authentic version of yourself.

FOCUS ON THE GOOD

One of the most transformational things we experience throughout our life is when we learn to focus on the good. People who focus on the good have an easier path to joy, fulfillment, happiness, and bliss in their lives. When we focus on the good, it's easier for us to be authentic, and when we stand in our authenticity, we understand we are unconditionally loved. You see the support available to you. You see how Source is working for you, instead of believing otherwise.

Your path will always feel easier when you focus on the good.

When you focus on the good, the good expands, and however cliché that may sound, it's an absolute truth. Source and your guides support you unconditionally. We are continuously guided and assisted on our journeys here. Your guides moving you on the path of the highest good, shifts the entire collective. This world is designed for making mistakes, for learning through really dense experiences—and we get to experience a whole host of higher vibrational experiences, like joy and love as well. Focus on the good—it allows you to experience *everything* from a higher perspective.

Gratitude is a life-changing practice.

It highlights the good in your present reality, allowing you to create from a place of unconditional love and alignment with the highest good. By focusing on what feels good, even when it seems like there's only a shred left, you tap into the power of your attention. In those moments, by choosing to focus on the good, it expands—maximizing your experience and shifting your perspective.

Developing a gratitude practice can feel so rudimentary and so simple in the beginning that we have a tendency to push it away. We write it off as something that will have minimal or no impact because it feels so simple. But that's one of the greatest lessons we have to learn here. *Small and simple things can make the biggest impact. Expanding* your understanding of the world requires reverence for how much the little things matter. The simple things, the things that don't cost a lot of time, money, or effort to do.

It's hard to believe that something as basic as a pen and a journal can transform your life, that writing down a few things you're grateful for every day can shift your entire reality.

But they absolutely can.

Gratitude reshapes not only your understanding of the world but also your sense of self.

Gratitude allows you to express the version of you that has been underneath the masks, trauma, and dense and difficult experiences all along. *The best part?* It works whether you believe it will or not. Simply committing to writing down your gratitude each day transforms your neural pathways and strengthens your soul's connection to the higher good. The practice itself carries the magic.

The practice shows us the smallest things have a massive impact. That it doesn't matter what your analytical mind thinks is possible. What Source has determined as possible is possible, whether you fully believe it or not. And when you practice it, the power of it is in the practice in and of itself. The practice of gratitude changes your neural networks and allows you to see the limitless possibilities and the impact of gratitude in your life.

I remember when I first started my gratitude practice. I didn't want to do it—I didn't believe that it was actually beneficial. I didn't believe it could have much of an impact. And when I committed to the process of writing down my gratitude and affirmations every day to rewire my neural networks, I began each entry with "I don't want to do this today."

I was honest about where I was. I was honest about what my belief level was—and I did it anyway. The people who were where I wanted to be swore gratitude was how they got there. So, I did it, even though my brain said it wouldn't work. Over time, I started to see more good. I started to feel better. I started to create more good in the world. Then I looked back and realized what an impact it had in my life over the first six months I practiced it. My life gained momentum in a positive direction, and I was able to look back and see how I dug myself out of a really dark place—piece by piece.

Practice gratitude for five years, and you will look back at your life and be shocked at how far you've come.

Practicing gratitude is the frequency of miracles.

Through the practice of gratitude, you gain the perspective of why everything had to happen the way that it happened. You become grateful for your difficult moments. You see how much they taught you. You see how much they gave you—what a gift all the challenges were and how they allowed for massive change in your life for the good.

When we feel like our light is dimming, gratitude brightens our soul.

Spend time every morning and every evening thinking about what you're grateful for. Commit to writing down what you're grateful for in combination with your positive affirmations and new beliefs once a day. When you commit your neural networks to gratitude, you completely rewire your brain to focus on the good.

When we rewire our brains with gratitude, we don't automatically see the negative in situations anymore. We change the lens with which we see the world. When something really dense happens, you're able to immediately find the good in it. You're able to see the lesson; you're able to see the purpose. You relax into knowing everything is always working out.

This shift makes you an agent of change in the world. It makes you the person that lights up a room. You're the person that lifts others up simply by being present—by doing nothing more than being yourself.

Gratitude is the entry point into a higher vibrational state. It's the doorway you have to walk through. Not every moment will feel good—nor is every moment going to go exactly how you planned. But when you sit in the vibrational space of gratitude, you see the benefit in things working out differently than you anticipated. You see there is a plan much bigger than your current understanding, and you allow yourself to flow to the places and spaces that you need to be to have the most beneficial experience for your soul. As you lean in to allowance through gratitude, you contribute to creating the higher good for all.

Sitting in a place of gratitude changes your frequency into authenticity.

When vibrating from a place of gratitude, you impact those around you by simply being around them. The frequency of gratitude is incredibly powerful, and when you sit in it continuously, it becomes so desirable to those around you, they start to walk toward it themselves. They become curious and figure out how to walk through the doorway of gratitude too. When you practice gratitude, you help others learn how to incorporate it into their own lives as well.

And that's why your gratitude practice isn't just for you, it's for everyone around you too. Gratitude has an exponential impact. It reverberates through the quantum energetic field. Changing the world is not about focusing on your problems. It's about focusing on the good you have. When you do, good exponentially grows.

As you embark on the journey of elevating into your authenticity through solidifying a gratitude practice, don't be surprised when resistance energies show up and attempt to deter you from the path. This is just the nature of the game, the way things are played here in this world. You have to move through denser energies to get to the higher vibrational ones. That means when you start working on yourself, resistance will show up internally and externally.

This isn't about being attacked or targeted spiritually. Be wary of any explanation of this process that incites fear. This process, at its core, is learning how to move through the resistance into a place that is free of it. It's a transformational journey, and you are learning and remembering how to alchemize energy as you go. When you transform resistance by focusing on the good, you reduce it, not only for yourself but for those that come after you on this journey.

The more you commit to a gratitude practice, the more elevated the baseline frequency of your experience will be.

Gratitude has a massive impact.

When resistance shows up, have an awareness of it. See it for what it is: not a barrier or a blockade but something you can simply choose to look at differently. When you choose to see the good, even in the face of the resistance, it takes the power away from the thing you feel you're up against. The resistance dissipates.

Where your focus goes, energy flows.

There will be layers of resistance as you move through your journey. Your layers of resistance are determined by the lessons you are working through—the themes of your life, the narratives that you are learning to overcome. Resistance is internal and external.

Your analytical mind will throw up resistance. Your nervous system will push back. Those you love and interact with resist new boundaries, not because you did anything wrong or because there's something "bad" happening but because your internal and external environments are currently structured to resist change.

If you're getting pushback in this process, you're moving in the right direction. You're doing the work that you need to do.

When you incorporate patience and become relentless with your connection to Faith, your ability to move through this process becomes clear, and the resistance dissipates over time.

I hear the phrase "that's easy to say but that's not easy to do" an awful lot as I share these teachings with the world. My response to that will always be "I know it's not easy. It's not supposed to be." Making these changes are the big impactful moments you will look back on and beam with pride—because they weren't easy. And just because something isn't easy doesn't make it impossible.

Learn to anticipate the difficulty; everything becomes a lot easier when you learn to view these challenges as something you are achieving, instead of something you are being punished with or victimized by. You become exponentially more powerful when you shift your perspective out of being a victim. That one perspective shift changes everything.

Committing to a gratitude practice allows you to sit in the vibration of gratitude while sitting in the frequency of change. This allows you to gain the perspective you need to see the world in a positive light as you move through the process of growth and healing.

The early stages of this process are more difficult—the early stages of learning anything new is more difficult. Changing your perspective and gaining momentum in a new direction isn't an easy thing to do. But it's not a process that lasts forever. Those initial stages of difficulty are not on an eternal loop. You will move on to different levels and new experiences that don't feel as difficult to move through.

Walk with Faith. You will not fail.

Focusing on the good means we have the opportunity to sit with the energy of Grace.

Grace is a feminine energy, and in her purest form, Grace is unconditional love. Including the unconditional love of self.

Grace helps you embody your worthiness. The truth is that we are all worthy—regardless of the mistakes we make. Grace sees past the limitations of our 3D reality on Earth and sees you for what you really are—Grace sees your soul. Allow yourself to sit in the energy of Grace—it will elevate you at the deepest levels of your being. Grace allows you to release limiting beliefs held deeply in your neural network, release stored trauma from the body, and connect with your authentic self.

Grace isn't something that's bestowed on us but an energy we walk with that we get to enjoy the presence of. *When I look at the energy of Grace, I see a good friend*—one who is happy to share her energy to help connect us more deeply to the depths of unconditional love. Unconditional love of self and of others. Grace is a multidimensional, angelic soul who will be there for you no matter what you do. She is ancient, she is ever present, and she's deeply connected to the unconditional love of Source.

Grace can show you that you deserve to be loved, that you deserve to be cared for, and that you deserve the best in life.

When I hear clients being hard on themselves, I always ask them if they would be so demanding and judgmental of someone who's close to them, that they love deeply. The answer is always no. Allow Grace to mirror that same level of understanding and care back to you. Life gets a lot easier when you do.

Source understood, as more and more souls became individual fractals of the whole, that we'd need the energy of Grace to understand what unconditional love is and how to embody it for ourselves. She'll find you in the darkest of places—she will show you your worth, your power, and your light—even when you can't see it for yourself. She will see you when no one else can.

We were all created to be exactly as we are. With the struggles we face, the challenges we meet, and the mistakes we make, and because of those mistakes, the lessons that cross our path teach us things. They allow us to forgive others and ourselves. They show us how to transmute energy—and they heal us through every version. They allow you to see that you're so much more than this lifetime and this place. No matter what you're faced with, the limitations you came into this world with, the family structure or lack thereof, or the traumas you've been dealt, Grace is waiting for you to sense she's there.

Grace will force you to look at yourself—giving you the opportunity to see your worth through your mistakes. She will show you how to accept what your heart knows to be true—you are love underneath all the layers.

Let me be clear: Grace will not give you an excuse to act in an unhealed manner. She will ask you to look in the mirror, to examine your mistakes, especially when you're terrified to do so. She will stand next to you as you look at what terrifies you the most, and she will help you face the decisions you've made and accept the consequences of your actions so that you may see how you can do better.

Grace allows you to see the moments where you are doing the best you can with what you have, and when you are truly falling short, she asks you to do better. Unconditional love is unconditional. When you face your mistakes and step up to the plate—taking responsibility for yourself, your life, your decisions—you stop repeating patterns of the past. That's where Grace will help you the most. *She sees who you can be, and she's pretty insistent that you get there.*

When you learn to let go of the versions of you that have been ingrained—the narratives you once believed were your personality, the beliefs you believed were just who you were, and the nervous system triggers that were the programs of how you behaved—you change your trajectory.

You become something different. Something free. At any moment you can choose to be something different—you can choose to act differently, and you can choose to step into your higher self.

You can choose to heal. And when you focus on the good, you understand that not a single thing is "perfect" in this reality. It's not supposed to be. That would create a world of sameness, and we're all supposed to be unique. We're supposed to have different experiences—we're supposed to learn to overcome the density and difficulty of this world as we do. We can't do that if we're perfect. If every time we try something new, we execute it flawlessly—there's no learning, no growth in that existence. It's a beautiful journey learning to accept the expansiveness of who you are. To go from a limited existence to an unlimited one.

Humans aren't the only ones that go through this process. We have visible representations of other transformations in this world. The butterfly is an excellent example of that, transforming through a chrysalis. They turn into a puddle of goo and reform into the beautiful butterflies we love. But in order for the caterpillar to survive the transformation, it has to have the courage to go into that chrysalis form and completely let go of everything they were to become their highest potential.

We have to do the same. The process looks a little different, but for the most part it's the same. And that's why we need Grace. She will be there—even when you've been temporarily turned to a pile of messy goo. She reminds you that you're loved—no matter how messy or uncomfortable you are.

It's time to allow yourself access to healed timelines of existence. Grace is waiting. Make mistakes, learn from them, and continue on.

On the topic of making mistakes and learning from them, Grace requires you to make and maintain healthy boundaries. The days of accepting less than what you deserve are over. Grace's energy provides the frequency you need to internalize self-worth. That means you will start to realize how important you are.

Your healing impacts others. When you heal, your frequency changes and that impacts everyone around you. *That's big stuff.* It's important to realize the healing work—on yourself—impacts others' healing. The only way to truly know where you fit in in this world and your particular flavor of genius is to lean in to your self-worth and hold healthy boundaries—everything else keeps you from reaching your potential.

Grace will insist that you walk away from the things that are limiting you. You will have to hold boundaries with the people who, regardless of the reason, aren't treating you right. You are worthy, and you need to embody your worth. She will show you all the pieces of your life that are out of alignment, and she will challenge you to take action to bring yourself into alignment.

Unconditional love is not unconditional access.

Perfectionism will not hold in the presence of Grace. Grace will force you to see where you are being too hard on yourself. Spending time beating yourself up and replaying events puts you in the energy of fear. Fear will keep you from taking steps on your path. You weren't built for your analytical mind's version of perfection. You were built to overcome—embody that.

It takes time to be really good at something. It takes practice—that's what makes it so rewarding—when you keep going. Grace will remind you how fun it is to find yourself. Dig in and follow your passions. Everything you try will not be in your highest alignment—that's part of learning discernment. *You can't know what's for you until you feel what isn't.*

Embodying self-worth with the help of Grace is an eye-opening experience. Grace showed me all the places and spaces I was short-changing myself—where I was accepting crumbs because I believed that's what I deserved. I lacked self-love. My self-worth was really low. I beat myself up for every mistake I made. I tried and failed at about a million things—and it left me feeling like I wasn't good at anything—when the reality was I gave up pretty quickly because I didn't believe in myself.

Grace saw me—the imperfect mess I was—and she insisted there was more potential there, if I allowed myself to see how worthy I was. Grace helped me elevate every area of my life, walking me home to myself. The process allowed me to embody a version of me who has unwavering self-love. A version who sees how amazing she is and sets her sights on the future appropriately . . . instead of settling for less. *Grace was with me through all of it.*

Call her in and ask for her help—she's waiting for the moment you are ready to see yourself. You are a beautiful fractal of the one collective consciousness. Walk with Grace and learn to express yourself. *Learn to love yourself.* Sometimes the most imperfect expressions of self are the most memorable, and you deserve to give yourself the opportunity to figure out what that is for you. Find your zone of genius—learn what makes you happy, lights you up, and brings you joy.

You are worthy of walking your path of discovery.

Move your perspective from the mistakes and the problems and simply focus on what you want the solution to be. *Focus on the good.*

Most of us don't need really specific things to be happy—we need higher emotional states. You need stability in those emotions, and you need to feel safe in those emotions. It's impossible to feel safe if your analytical mind is the one beating you up all the time. Make time to work on your beliefs. Create safety in yourself, and you will meet all that you are.

Grace is a force to be reckoned with—invite her into your life. She will show you how much space you are being given to be you.

Let the internal resistance to your authenticity go.

She is your guide as much as she is mine.

You've got this. Keep going.

CHAPTER 7

THE EMOTIONAL BODY

The emotional body affects every area of your life. Emotional triggers fire and wire our nervous system and set the vibrational tone of the manifestations we draw into us. As the sum of our lived experiences, the emotional body has a direct influence on our energetic body.

One of the most important ways we transmute energy is by processing emotions. Emotions, when felt, are energy in motion. *When felt is the key here.* When you ignore or suppress emotions, they stop moving, and they become trapped within the body—waiting for you to feel and process them. Over time, stored emotions affect not only your vibration but also your physical health, creating blockages in your tissues, muscles, fascia, and fat cells. The life systems are interconnected—when we heal emotional aspects, we bring healing to our other life systems as well.

Fortunately, conscious awareness isn't always needed to process our emotions. And while emotions are a part of memories, we don't need a remembrance of every event tied to every emotion to process our emotional state. This is an important aspect to understand if you've had deep emotional trauma that you are fearful of revisiting. Not all wounds need to be reopened to be healed. We also process the emotional load from our bloodline's unprocessed past. The latest research suggests we carry 7 to 14 generations of information from our genetic line—giving us the opportunity to provide healing for the generations of souls ill-equipped to complete the process themselves.

The emotional body impacts your physical body more than you realize. The emotions left unprocessed store themselves in your body tissue. While muscles, fascia, and fat cells store the majority of our unprocessed emotions, it's important to understand that any cell in the body can carry emotional information. Emotions are tied to neural networks that are integrated into every area of your body. This is why you are able to feel your emotions in a deep, visceral way.

Healing often begins by learning how to feel, and feel deeply. By doing the work of emotional healing, you release trapped energy, whether or not you remember the original cause. The release of energy moves across all levels of your being. Every time you feel your emotions, you expand your capacity to feel more, growing your soul's understanding of the possibilities of life.

The emotional body is one of the major reasons we come to Earth.

As a soul, the capacity for feeling and connecting the way we do in a human body is a unique experience. The range of emotional experience on Earth is vast. Which is why our human body is entangled with the emotional body as much as it is. We can embody physical healing through gratitude—and we can die of a broken heart. This spectrum of experience provides soul growth.

Spectrum of Experience

Love
Gratitude
Peace
Freedom
Joy
Happiness
Enthusiasm
Contentment
Optimism

AS ABOVE

Boredom

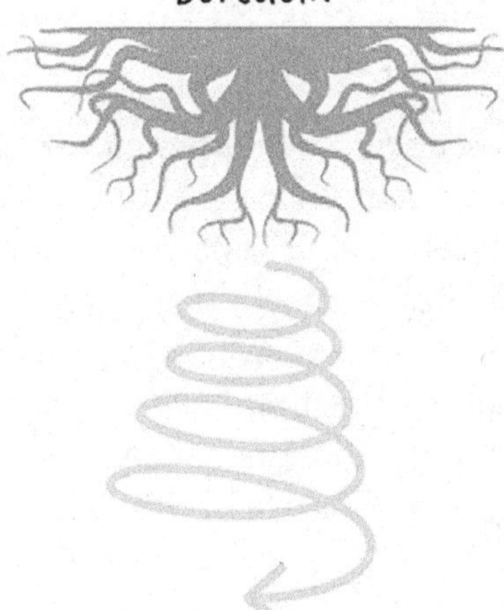

So Below

Pessimism
Pride
Anger
Rage
Jealousy
Fear
Insecurity
Guilt
Shame

Feeling isn't easy—initially. We often mistake our current state of emotions for who we are. But they aren't who we are. Emotions are energies you are meant to move through, shifting your energy from place to place, emotion to emotion, acknowledging each emotion and feeling as you go.

Feeling, as deeply as you can, allows you to move emotional energy up and out of the body, causing an energetic release that propels transformation. Every emotion you face, every time you have the guts to feel, you expand your capacity, your container of energy. The more you feel, the more powerful you become.

There will be times where you will sit in the dark, feeling the depths of really dense emotions. But these moments of heaviness expand your capacity to fill with light. Your ability to feel and process dense emotions is directly proportional to your ability to feel the lighter ones. Your depth determines your height. Just like a tree can only grow as tall and wide as its roots will support, you're anchored by your ability to feel.

We build just as many coping mechanisms for feeling "good" as we do for feeling "bad."

Feeling deeply—whether we interpret it as positive or negative—is uncomfortable. Feeling emotions can be so uncomfortable that we will deploy a host of self-sabotaging behaviors and coping mechanisms when we feel "good" just as much, if not more, than when we feel "bad." The reason we have coping mechanisms and self-sabotaging behavior at all is because we're afraid to feel—good, bad, or otherwise.

Healing through the emotional body is learning how to feel, embody, and express emotions in a healthy and productive way. Feeling our emotions is something we are learning how to do as a collective as well. When you improve your capacity to feel and process emotions, you heal—expanding consciousness through the increase in your capacity.

Souls brought into this world now come in with a larger capacity and a greater understanding of emotional processing than their predecessors had. Their baseline is sitting at a higher frequency due to the work the collective is doing. The elevated baseline creates a greater depth of feeling—lending to a greater awareness of what and who we actually are. When we understand humanness better, it's clear we are not our emotions. *They are a gift of experience.*

This world is one of the few places in the universe with such a depth of feeling. When you integrate this into your understanding, you shift your perspective to one of gratitude for the emotions you feel. With this shift, you process emotions quickly because there's joy in it. You realize that it's an incredible experience to feel anything at all.

By leaning in to the depths of the emotional experience available to you, you release your fear of the unknown. You come to understand that there is always a choice between love and lack, and you can always choose love—creating our reality from that space.

When we embrace the experience of feeling, we shorten the period we sit in dense emotions while increasing the time we spend in the higher states. I call this the refractory period—the time it takes us to move from one vibrational state to another.

Lean in to loving the emotions you experience. You'll be surprised at how fast you move through the denser emotions when you do.

UNDERSTANDING EMOTIONS

We all experience triggering emotions—high highs and low lows. These emotional waves can take us back to memories and experiences that have deeply impacted us from this lifetime and many others. Though dealing with emotions doesn't always feel like a blessing, especially with the denser ones, it is. Understanding emotions allows us to see and understand ourselves better. And when we recognize emotions are temporary, and not the entirety of who we are, we move through them with speed and ease we didn't know was possible.

Emotions are vibrational frequencies—energy in motion when we keep them moving. And as such, they act as magnets, attracting and pushing things away. When we begin to understand the sum of our stored emotions is the vibrational resonance we put out into the world, we can influence our energy more effectively. Acting on this awareness gives us the power to align our vibration with our highest self, not only for ourselves but also for the collective good.

We come to Earth to experience a wide range of emotions. In other realms there are more solid states of frequency, emotional frequency that exists in continual sameness or solely on a collective level versus an individual level. When we exist in a state of continual sameness, we don't have the same opportunities to expand our soul growth as we do here, where we are working with a wide range of emotional frequencies, in the depths and the heights.

Since emotions operate as frequencies, it's important to understand that they exist on a spectrum—both in vibration and intensity. We can experience emotions intensely and deeply, but the intensity of the emotional experience isn't determined by the amount of time we spend in the emotion but the amplitude of the wave of energy the emotion is experienced at. Amplitude is the strength of the wave.

With practice and awareness, you can learn to feel emotions deeply without being overwhelmed by them.

We can experience a multitude of emotions at the same time, and as we gain awareness with ourselves, we have an easier time identifying the emotions that we experience. When working on understanding emotions, awareness is a huge factor. Awareness is your key to understanding emotions—knowing not only what you're feeling but why you're feeling it. *If it's a triggering emotion, what triggered you? Why did it trigger you?* A lot of times, what you'll find is that you end up seeing an emotional cord from your current experience back to something from a previous experience. Seeing and feeling the cord allows you to release it—freeing you from the automatic responses attached to it.

In some cases, a simple acknowledgment of an emotion will provide a release—while others require a deeper understanding. Which emotions we need an understanding of and those we can easily release is completely dependent on you and the parameters your soul requires for growth. It's important to understand the depth with which we can feel dense emotions is directly proportional to the height we can go into the elevated ones. Our highs are defined by our lows.

> ***Feeling emotions provides growth for the soul.***

It's part of mastering the human experience. We came here to learn, to grow, and evolve as souls. Through your experiences, you learn to transmute emotions, feel them fully, and release them. In doing so, you shift from programmed emotional responses to choosing conscious reactions. You align with your true desires and potential in these shifts.

Emotions are frequencies we *get to* experience. Feel the freedom in that.

Learning to understand our emotions looks different for everyone. It's a deeply introspective process. Where we feel emotions in our body, how we feel them, the triggers we have, are all a unique experience. There's generalizations we can make about the healing process—but the individual steps we take on the path of healing look different for each of us.

Embracing this authentic process upfront is really important. Everyone will have different experiences they've stored that they're processing, and when we fall into the trap of comparing our journey to others, our analytical minds can convince us we are behind or lacking in some way. This is a deeply internal journey.

For some, the process of freeing oneself of emotional triggers runs incredibly deep. There's trauma to process—current life trauma and past life trauma, stored and carried through time and space. But the preverbal baggage we carry gets processed only when we have the capacity to do so.

For others, emotional processing can feel more surface level. Past life experiences may have been processed within those lives, leading to us coming into this lifetime with a lighter load. Souls with less experience will also have less to process as they have less stored emotional experiences to transmute.

Learning your emotional triggers and what pulls your emotional attention is incredibly important.

When we're triggered into an emotion, it's not an autonomous decision. It's an automatic reaction, a programmed response. Emotional triggers are a physiological response you learn to free yourself from—the more triggers you free yourself from, the more freedom you have, creating the space you need to step into your authentic self. When a trigger is fully processed, it no longer elicits the same emotional response you were once conditioned to.

The more triggers we are exposed to, and subsequently process, the closer to our authentic alignment we get. Being triggered is an opportunity to heal. You alter your life trajectory when you choose differently in the face of the obstacles and triggers that had previously defined your path. When you reprogram and process those experiences, you release them from your emotional system, forming new neural networks and automatic responses to the stimuli in your environment that you want, instead of what you don't. This frees you to sit in the vibration of the future you desire.

We aren't defined by emotions, but our life is a result of how we react to them.

The more we understand our emotions, the more we detach from them, the more we understand emotions are a temporary experience. No matter how good or bad you feel an experience is . . . it is temporary.

I've worked with a lot of clients that have had amazingly profound mystical experiences. Mystical experiences, in many circumstances, can provide the emotional vibration of unconditional love and bliss, a feeling that can be overwhelming and all-consuming while it is being felt. What I've found is once this feeling is experienced, many who've felt it feel a loss initially when they're not consistently sitting in that emotional state.

Releasing attachment includes allowing the highly elevated experiences to ebb and flow as much as the other emotions.

Emotions teach us to be grateful for every moment. They are meant to constantly move and travel through us. You maximize your experience when you feel without attachment, allowing things to flow. Understanding the impermanence of emotions gives you the ability to create an elevated experience of ease, joy, peace, and freedom. You learn to understand the experience of loss, grief, and other dense emotions will pass, creating more ease in your life.

Low-vibrational emotions are simply a mirror to the higher ones.

They create the contrast we need to increase our depth of experience in this world. When we understand this, we allow ourselves to process our experience faster—moving into higher vibrational states—shortening the refractory period in the denser stuff.

Learn to love all the emotional experiences, and you will find freedom.

SHADOW WORK

Shadow work is one of our greatest allies when healing the emotional body. And it's also one of the most misunderstood ways to heal.

We often forget that our shadow self is born from the light—created by it. The light needs the dark to understand itself. And it's through this contrast—of the lighter and darker pieces—we learn to understand ourselves, gaining a deeper awareness of who we are and the experiences that have shaped us.

Shadow work gives us access to the depths of the density we've experienced. It allows you to confront your mistakes and understand the motivations behind the actions you're not proud of. And you get the opportunity to explore and release the emotions you've experienced, making room for fully integrated versions of yourself.

It takes courage to face the parts of yourself you've kept hidden in the shadows—the places where you hold pain, fear, and shame around being seen.

But when you shed light into the dark corners, you show yourself it's safe to accept what was, freeing you to move forward. Every shadow you explore reclaims the fragmented parts of your soul, turning what once felt broken into a beautiful expression of self and turning your fear of darkness into reverence.

We can see a representation of this process through *Kintsugi*—the Japanese art of repairing broken objects with a gold lacquer. The practice is meant to remind us that we can create something more beautiful with the fractured pieces through the act of bringing them back together. Just as plants begin their growth underground in dense, dark places, our soul requires the same conditions for growth. *No mud, no lotus.*

Through shadow work, you learn to transmute dense energy into light, gaining an awareness of your own capacity to turn darkness into beautiful experiences. While shadow work can feel terrifying, it's also liberating. It reveals the hidden aspects of yourself—the part of your ego raging against the light. We have to see all of ourselves to love who we are. You don't get to pick and choose which parts of you to love.

Part of the bargain of being you is accepting and loving all of you.

Shadow aspects can come forward when triggered in social interactions, episodes of anxiety, sadness, and in relationships. Your shadow contains repressed emotions from traumatic and painful events, and these repressed emotions formed neural networks in the form of limiting beliefs—which result in impulsive and undesirable behavior.

Your shadow self is the discarded, abandoned, and repressed pieces of self you've deemed unlovable, unacceptable, and unworthy. Shadow work is the process of accepting and integrating the parts of yourself you've rejected, and it's the process of healing the wounds that caused you to cast pieces of yourself to the side to begin with.

When you learn to accept what has happened in your life, you free yourself from the shadow, giving you the opportunity to put yourself back together in an even more beautiful way.

I like to see shadow work as a scavenger hunt. Life events cause us to lose pieces of ourselves, and it's our job to gather those discarded soul fragments. When we've gathered them, we get to accelerate expanding our consciousness. Going on a scavenger hunt in the shadows to bring all of our soul pieces home is an adventure. It's an integral part of our mission and purpose here on Earth.

Reclaiming our fragments helps us see our triggers and identify the toxic behavior patterns we've been running. With awareness, we can heal, remove triggers, and create healthy behavior patterns instead. You also end up finding out what you care about the most. Our wounds have a tendency to show us what our soul needs and is drawn to. Going into the shadow space is part of your purpose. *There's nowhere the light is needed more than in the darkness.*

It's important to set intentions before beginning shadow work. Setting an intention to be open and compassionate of what you may find is an important part of the work. It's hard to look into a mirror that shows all sides of ourselves. Shadow work requires you to examine the moments where you were not kind, where you chose unhealthy patterns over healing, where you acted out of alignment with your integrity.

Have the courage to view these moments as an observer, as someone who is willing to accept what was and is willing to learn and grow from what you find. This will elevate you on your journey. It can be incredibly painful to seek out and heal these parts of ourselves. It's important to process any shame, guilt, and judgment that floats forward while you move through the shadow space. Processing and releasing these dense emotions allows you to reintegrate your soul fragments. *You can heal and come home to yourself.*

Shame creates more density than anything else—and this is where your most elusive soul pieces will hide, where you feel abandoned and unlovable. While these will be the hardest places to explore, remember that the depths with which you allow yourself to experience these emotions are directly proportional to the heights you can go in the higher vibrational spaces. Go in, gather yourself, and get out. You're not meant to live in the darkness.

Shadow work is a rescue mission.

You are your own hero—find your way out.

PHYSICAL MANIPULATION OF EMOTION

When healing the emotional body, we have to acknowledge how deeply it's connected to the physical body. Unprocessed emotions are stored in our tissue—which means there will be times we will need to release them through physical manipulation of the body.

Physical manipulation is vital for emotional healing. When we go in search of our soul fragments in the shadow spaces, it's very common for the body to react. Pain and discomfort can arise when removing emotions from the body. We release physically just as much as we do emotionally.

Emotions are meant to move. When they become trapped and immobilized, it can hurt to remove them from the places they've been trapped. Our physical body did its best to adapt to their presence. The body made adjustments in metabolism and the immune system to compensate for the storage of these emotions. And as the body releases these emotions, it will go through a detox period, recalibrating to receive higher vibrations.

Some common physical symptoms that coincide with emotional healing are exhaustion, muscle aches and pains, muscle soreness, muscle twitching, back and hip pain, headaches, migraines, flu-like symptoms, digestive issues, changes in appetite, changes in body weight, and generalized pain. This is a normal—and an uncomfortable—part of the process.

Fascial maneuvers, restorative yoga, deep stretching, and foam rolling are all ways you can support moving stored emotions out of the body. Lean in to understanding how connected your emotional and physical system is and utilize the tools available to you to heal. These forms of physical manipulation help move emotions out of the body, often bringing stored emotions to the surface even when we aren't consciously trying to release them. It's also not unusual to experience emotional responses during these sessions without fully understanding where the emotions are coming from.

The good news is we don't need a conscious understanding of where the emotions are coming from to process them. Our only job is to face what shows itself. If an understanding is required to process an emotion, one will present itself. It's productive to cry through a physical manipulation session without knowing why. *Crying is a way for the physical body to release emotion.* The tears won't flow heavy forever, but please be mindful of the dam you've built and the reservoir you're holding back. We were meant to keep our emotions flowing; the dam has to go.

We will dive deeper into healing the physical body in the next section—for now, accept and integrate the fact that you have stored emotions in your tissue. Muscle, facia, skin, and fat all carry biological and emotional memory. Physical manipulation allows you to understand your emotional storage capacity—set intentions for release and take the necessary action you need to take to let go of your emotional reserves.

The pain is temporary—move it up and out of you.

You've got this. Keep going.

CHAPTER 8

THE PHYSICAL BODY

Bargains are one of the oldest forms of magic—ancient agreements made with Source. These contracts bind us to the terms we agreed upon, and if we fail to fulfill our end of the bargain, Source will complete the contract in other ways. Bringing your soul into a physical body on Earth is part of the bargain of gaining experience here. Taking care of your body and understanding how it works is part of this. While we are not defined by our physical form, we were provided this vessel as a vehicle while we're here, which means we need reverence for it and to take care of it.

When we neglect our physical body, our energetic body, emotional body, and mental body are all impacted. Everything is connected; the health of one life system will influence the others.

Being bound to this body while we're here means we need to understand how it works. And while we come screaming into this world without an operating manual for the body, we can remember how to best take care of it and move through the world with it. If you listen carefully, the body will teach you how to care for your physical home. You can develop open communication with your body through the signals it provides.

Your responsibility is clear: You need to fuel the body appropriately, move it regularly, cleanse it, and, most importantly, love it. Just as all living things are connected to Source Consciousness, our body is too. Our bodies understand the terms we accepted entering this realm, and while the body doesn't have a soul the way we are a soul in the body, the body is connected to Source.

The binding of your soul to your physical body is your entrance and exit point for this world.

The body is the form anchoring you into the three-dimensional reality you are experiencing. It's your personal form of transportation, allowing you to experience the world through your senses. It's also the portal that we can bring more souls into this world with.

Like our other systems, the body is electrical and functions at its best when energy flows freely. It's your job to learn your optimal ranges for sleep, stress, movement, and energy intake. The more mindful you are of how you care and connect with your body, the better it serves you in life.

Your body is influenced by both your internal environment—your thoughts, emotions, and energy—and external factors, including the people you surround yourself with. We store emotional baggage within the body and our energy field is continuously affecting the body systems. Our body will alert us to issues, but we tend to ignore the signals before we wake up to all that we are. During meditation, we can evaluate what our body is saying—the same way we listen for cues of what is happening in our mental, emotional, and energetic life systems.

Your body understands the experiences you are meant to explore and how long you are meant to be in the body.

These experiences were agreed upon when you bound yourself to your physical form—they govern your entrance and exit from this life. While we may believe we have control over the extension or shortening of our time here, the truth is Source holds the contract of how long we are here. Accepting this truth will allow you to release the illusion of control and live in alignment with your highest, most authentic self. While you already agreed to your amount of time in your body—you can maximize your experience through actualizing your potential. Learn to work with the body instead of fighting it.

The physical experience deserves your reverence and the body can help you greatly if you learn to honor the partnership you made.

THE NERVOUS SYSTEM

The nervous system comes up a lot when we are working on releasing limiting beliefs, toxic behavior patterns, and low-vibrational emotional patterns.

What is the nervous system?

In short, the nervous system is your body's command center. It starts in your brain and forms a complex system of nerve connections throughout your entire body.

Your nervous system affects every aspect of your being, including:

- Thoughts, memory, learning, and feelings
- All movement, including balance and coordination
- All your senses, including how your brain interprets what you see, hear, taste, touch, and feel
- Sleep amount and quality, healing, and aging
- Breathing and heartbeat
- How we respond to stressful situations
- Digestion, including hunger and thirst
- Hormone regulation and life cycle stages
- Pain levels and pain tolerance

The nervous system not only affects your physical response to your environment but also plays a massive role in your perception of it. The nervous system's vast network of nerves sends electrical signals to and from cells, glands, and muscles all over our body. These nerves receive information from everything around you—interpreting the information and controlling your response to stimuli.

The nervous system is a massive information highway covering your entire body. How well we regulate our nervous system determines how happy we are, how we handle stressful situations, and if we are able to navigate through the world as our higher self.

While the nervous system isn't who we are as spiritual beings, the nervous system is the wiring operating the body. Every programmed limiting belief, every unresolved trauma, every health aliment, and every memory and your interpretation of those experiences moves through the nervous system.

Learning to regulate your nervous system gives you the power to create new responses to your internal and external environment.

A regulated nervous system is needed for higher vibrational behavior as it controls the way we experience our senses. *When you heal your nervous system, your perspective of the world shifts.* The nervous system is the electrical system moving energy through the body. The amount of energy you move, how it's flowing, and the frequency of it dictate your behavior and how you feel.

The nervous system has two main parts, with each part containing billions of cells called neurons or nerve cells. These cells pass energy between each other, and where the energy ends up dictates how your body responds.

The first part of the nervous system is the *central nervous system.* This is your brain and spinal cord. The second part is the *peripheral nervous system.* This is the massive network of nerves running throughout the entire body, relaying signals to and from the *central nervous system.*

The *peripheral nervous system* contains the *somatic nervous system,* which controls voluntary movements, and your *autonomic nervous system,* which controls everything you do without thinking (like breathing and your heartbeat). When I talk about the fight-or-flight response and your ability to subsequently calm down from that, I am referring to the *autonomic nervous system.* This system is the main focus of your regulation practice.

The autonomic nervous system breaks down into three main parts.

1. **Sympathetic nervous system:** The system that activates in times of stress or danger. This is the system responsible for *fight-or-flight.*
2. **Parasympathetic nervous system:** The system responsible for calming you down and getting you into the rest-and-digest state. This is the area controlled mainly by the vagus nerve. So, if you hear people talking about treatments that involve vagus nerve stimulation, these are treatments designed to stimulate the *parasympathetic nervous system.*
3. **Enteric nervous system:** The part of the nervous system that manages how our body digests food. Regulating the nervous system will affect digestive disorders. An unregulated nervous system can cause all kinds of digestive disorders, malabsorption, metabolism issues, and things like IBS.

The autonomic nervous system impacts every area of your life.

It affects how you see the world and your reaction to it. Your health and well-being is impacted deeply by your nervous system, and learning to regulate it can greatly impact your health. Many autoimmune diagnoses are effectively resolved with nervous system and emotional healing.

Learning how to operate and care for your body is part of the spiritual experience. Doing so elevates your conscious understanding of the interconnectedness of all things and actions.

REGULATING THE NERVOUS SYSTEM

Nervous system regulation is, at its core, the ability to move flexibly between different states of arousal in response to stressors.

Proper regulation means that when you encounter a change in your environment, like a stressful situation, you can adapt so that you are not overwhelmed. It also means you completely recover after the stressor has been removed. Unfortunately, until we learn the proper techniques, we are unable to switch between stress and relaxation. Our environment is highly stimulating for the nervous system, and if we were to compare the nervous system to the drive system in a vehicle, it's like the nervous system gets stuck in drive versus being able to shift into neutral, reverse, and park.

Being able to flex between these states is really important for health, well-being, and your interpretation of our world. The ability to be flexible and adapt to the circumstances gives you a sense of agency; it makes you feel confident and secure because you can understand and navigate the world in the way you choose. When your nervous system is regulated, being in your body fosters a sense of safety. When your nervous system isn't regulated properly, you'll feel overwhelmed, which translates into a sense of powerlessness—the space where you feel you have no control over how you respond to triggers, and you remain stuck in responses even after the trigger is removed. When your nervous system is chronically misregulated, your body develops various symptoms and conditions. Being in a body with a misregulated nervous system may feel painful, uncomfortable, or even terrifying.

Trauma, burnout, illness, and chronic pain all stem from an overwhelmed nervous system.

The nervous system is the foundation of our lived experience, connecting our body and mind and regulating our emotional and mental state, immune system, and every other body system. The nervous system connects you with the environment around you, allowing you to relate to other beings and enabling your spiritual understanding.

This interconnectedness means that when we are struggling to cope with anxiety, illness, emotional pain, burnout, and trauma, we need to address all parts of being human if we want deep, long-lasting healing.

A regulated nervous system requires care for each of the life systems.

The energetic, mental, emotional, and physical bodies all play into a regulated nervous system. We often get frustrated or blocked in our healing journey because initially, it can be hard to grapple with the fact that physical symptoms could be due to a problem that isn't rooted in the physical. However, if we take a step back and look at every part of us, we start to see that a physical symptom can be a messenger of something deeper, and we can work on these different components of the human experience to achieve true, long-lasting healing.

Western medicine is slow to accept the intersection of our mental, emotional, energetic, and physical body, but the conversation around the nervous system, its function, and how we find lasting healing is beginning to shift toward addressing the whole person, not just the symptom or the condition.

We come into this world with varying levels of sensitivity built into our nervous system. Your genetics play a role in determining your degree of sensitivity, and the genetics you have are determined by the agreements you made with Source to gain your body.

A highly sensitive nervous system will be highly sensitive to energy.

And while being highly sensitive is a spiritual gift, it comes with the cost of putting in extra effort to regulate the nervous system. *Spiritual gifts require responsibility.* They aren't awarded by Source without a counterbalance involved. Your greatest challenges point directly to your gifts. Learning to regulate the nervous system is part of the spiritual path. Environmental factors like our upbringing, societal background, relationships, and personal history are all known variables in our ability to regulate. Your nervous system is a combination of everything you've ever experienced and everything you need to learn to elevate.

Neuroplasticity is the scientific term for the reprogramming work we do on the nervous system. And while the healing work required to do it isn't easy, the nervous system can absolutely be reset and reprogrammed. Remember, there are going to be points in your journey where aligning with Faith is required.

Reprogramming often forces us to face the traumas our nervous system experienced, and while trauma is often thought of as a major one-off event, there can be sets of events happening to us over time causing the programmed reactions. Trauma can be caused by overwhelming, violent events, such as abuse, neglect, and horrifying experiences in our internal and external environments, but they can also be caused by objectively smaller things like being rejected from a friend circle or being bullied as a child.

Trauma has less to do with what happened to you and more to do with how your nervous system processed and made meaning of what happened.

How the events were interpreted by the nervous system determines the impact more than the events themselves. One of the most important things we can do on our healing journey is to work on building a coherent narrative of our life so we can allow our analytical mind to make sense of our past and present experiences, trauma included. This will help you understand your current circumstances and what experiences formed the current expression of who you are.

Access memories and experiences from a place of nonjudgment. Approach healing work from a place of curiosity, where you can gather information without making any judgment about what was right, wrong, or otherwise. That space is where we have the most success.

The most common problem I see when people are working to heal themselves is they give up too soon. Most will try one tool or tip they've acquired and see improvements for a bit. Then a cycle of misregulation pops up, the nervous system fights the change, and they move away from Faith and back to fear.

You are not broken.

Nervous system regulation takes time to see results. Remind yourself to be patient and feel the force of Faith when the ups and downs inevitably show up. Learn to ride the wave of the nervous system's response.

The body will fight change—not because it's fighting you but because the neural networks causing the misregulation run deep. It will be physically and mentally uncomfortable. Decide what your motivation is before you start the process and hold on to it for dear life in the difficult moments.

We all need a reason to keep going. Find yours.

The more you regulate your nervous system, the easier it gets. First you develop an awareness for your body sensations and emotions. You gain an understanding of how your body feels when your nervous system is pushing you into a response, and you learn how to respond to the stressors in a healthy way. Having a collection of regulation tools and using them over time allows you to reverse the damage to your nervous system and forge a new path.

Tool 1: Use Your Breath

Deep breathing effectively regulates the nervous system. Every time you take a deep breath, you contract your diaphragm, and when this occurs, the vagus nerve is stimulated. The vagus nerve is the main driver of getting you into the rest-and-digest state brought on by stimulating the parasympathetic nervous system.

Not all breathing techniques work the same, and my personal preference for regulating the nervous system is a 7-7-7-7 breathing method.

To complete this breathing technique, inhale slowly for a count of seven, hold for a count of seven, exhale slowly for a count of seven, hold at the bottom for seven, and repeat as many times as you need to fully come out of a heightened state. Use this breathing technique anytime you feel stressed, are struggling with poor self-talk, feel dense feelings rising up, or simply need to check in with yourself.

Slowing down to focus on the breath will provide you with a feeling of peace in chaotic situations. Focusing on the breath pulls you out of your mind and into your body. Focusing on the breath reduces anxiety, bringing you back to the present moment.

Breath is life. Bring your attention back to it. Your life will change because of this practice.

Tool 2: Shock Your System with Cold Exposure

Cold exposure is an excellent way to regulate the nervous system as it triggers the vagus nerve to turn on the rest-and-digest state as well.

A cold plunge practice or cryotherapy can be used regularly if that is available to you. Significant changes in how the nervous system responds can be accomplished in as little as 7 to 11 minutes of cold exposure per week. Adding one to two minutes of cold exposure a day is all that's needed for a nervous system benefit.

Plunge pools and cryotherapy aren't always an available or cost-effective method. Adding a cold-water practice to the end of a shower is. The nervous system needs to be pulled back into a relaxed state by the vagus nerve, consistently, to have a lasting effect. Incorporating a cold-water practice into a daily hygiene practice is an easy and effective way to accomplish two tasks at once. One to two minutes is all that's needed per session.

There are moments where you'll find yourself in a heightened state that will need immediate regulation. In these moments, an ice pack is a great option. Placing an ice pack on the chest and the back of the neck will stimulate the vagus nerve, causing the body to relax. Cold exposure can also be done on the face alone. This practice can be done with ice packs on the face or by taking a bowl of ice water and submerging the face for as long as you can hold your breath. I've even seen some dedicated users of this practice with a snorkel to increase their length of exposure.

Stimulating the vagus nerve regularly makes the nervous system highly flexible, which is exactly what you want for proper regulation.

Tool 3: Tap It Out

Tapping on various acupressure points on the body calms the nervous system, reducing anxiety and stress. For this practice, use your index and middle fingers to tap on the body's meridian points five to seven times on each point.

The meridian points are as follows:

- Start of the eyebrow above the nose
- Outer side of the eye below the eyebrows
- Under the eye
- Under the nose
- Divot below lower lip
- Two inches below the collar bone (often tender to touch)
- Under the arm about four inches down
- Top of the head, in the middle

Repeat the full cycle, moving through the meridian points, until a state of calm in the mind and body is achieved.

Tool 4: Gain Flexibility with Meditation

Meditation is incredibly important for regulating the nervous system. Making the time each day to quiet the mind and allow for the growth of a deep spiritual connection helps manage your energy day-to-day and long-term. Meditation also helps to locate, move, and regulate stored energy in the body, energy in the form of trauma and pain.

Meditation allows you to heal from these energies, creating the space for higher-frequency energy to enter your body, connecting you with your higher self.

Meditation is the overarching treatment to the underlying problems with the nervous system.

Without meditation, navigating regulation of the nervous system is quite difficult. Meditation is our foundational practice and must be used with the other regulation strategies to be effective.

I recommend specific meditation methods that allow for reprogramming, balancing, and creating brain and heart coherence. Meditations like *The Awakening Series* are available on my website. These meditations allow you to alter your brain frequency, which gives you access to the deepest parts of your consciousness. Accessing the deepest parts of your awareness provides great insight into the expansiveness of all you are. Meditation also gives you access to the root of your limiting beliefs. Most people will move through their day in a brainwave frequency called beta. The analytical mind runs well in the beta frequency. Meditations that move our energy and brains into alpha or theta frequencies give us better access to the deeper spaces, like the subconscious and the quantum realm.

Surface-level meditations will provide a calming and less reactive feeling, but we have to access altered frequency states in the brain for deep reprogramming of the mind and nervous system. Committing to a meditation practice is an important part of the spiritual path. The meditative space is where you can actively heal and accept quantum assistance from high-vibrational energies.

Tool 5: Move Your Body

Deep stretching, dancing, and shaking stimulate the vagus nerve. Move the body to music and visualize stress leaving the body through your movements. Shake your arms and legs.

Feel the energy of stress leaving your body. Find fun and creative ways to move and embrace gratitude for the physical experience.

You can learn to operate your physical form with ease—but it requires action on your part to do the regulation work in the moments that make you a master. Invest the energy in yourself.

Now that we've tended to the foundation—your energy, your mind, your emotions, and your body—you're no longer simply surviving an awakening into your authenticity. You're building the stability to hold the expansion you came here for. *Regulate* gave you the tools to return to your center, regardless of the chaos and intensity of the world.

But the real magic? That happens when you *live* from this regulated state. This is when all the practices, the inner work, the nervous system rewiring take hold and it shows up in how you move through your day, your relationships, your decisions, your boundaries, and how you hold yourself.

That's where you *integrate* what you've learned.

It's time to *live* what you've remembered.

You've got this. Keep going.

PART III

Integrate

Transformation is a continuous journey that unfolds with each choice, each breath, and each moment of courage. The process of awakening and healing is like planting seeds—the integration part is where those seeds, buried in the depths of the soil, take root and bloom. It's the sacred space where we take everything we've learned and begin to weave it into the fabric of who we are. Integration is the space between knowing and becoming—a deliberate act of aligning with our higher selves.

Pause and reflect on how far you've come already. The path you walked wasn't easy, yet here you are. You've faced your shadows, confronted beliefs that once held you back, and glimpsed the vastness of your own potential. But now, the real work begins. Awareness is only the first step; transformation takes root in how you embody what you've uncovered.

Integration asks us to sit in both the beauty and the discomfort of change. It invites you to step into the life you're creating, not as an abstract idea but as a fully lived reality. It's the difference between dreaming of the person you're becoming and waking up each day living as them.

Integration is the process of taking insights and revelations and transforming them into a way of being.

It's not just remembering the lessons you've learned—it's about becoming them. Integration is where the mind and the heart converge, and where truths are grounded into the unshakable foundation of your core.

Picture this: You've climbed a mountain. You feel the burn in your muscles and the exhilaration of the climb in your chest as you reach the summit. The ascent was full of lessons—resilience, determination, surrender. But the journey doesn't end just because you reach the top. The real transformation happens on the way down. You carry the lessons with you and let them shape how you move through the world. Integration is that descent. It's where wisdom is embodied, not just understood.

Learning opens the door, but integration invites you to walk through it. It bridges the gap between the intellectual awareness of your potential and the lived experience of that potential. It's not enough to understand the concept of self-love; integration is showing yourself kindness when it feels hardest. It's not enough to know your worth; integration is standing firm in it when others challenge it.

Transformation begins with a spark—an insight, a breakthrough, a moment of drastic change.

But without integration, that spark can fade, leaving us just as we were. Integration is the alchemy that turns those sparks into an eternal flame. It's the work of taking what you've learned and letting it bleed into your choices, your relationships, and your identity.

This phase of the journey isn't always easy. Integration will reveal its own set of challenges. You might feel resistance to leaving behind old patterns, even the ones that no longer serve you. You might face setbacks that make you question whether you've grown at all. These moments aren't signs you've failed the healing journey—in fact they're opportunities to solidify your transformation.

Every time you choose alignment over comfort, every time you lean in to love instead of lack, you are integrating a higher alignment.

Integration isn't perfect. There will be days when you slip back into old ways. This is human. This is normal. Integrating requires that you continue to show up again and again—with compassion for yourself when you make mistakes. Faith is always there to guide you. This journey will show you time and time again that it's progress, not perfection, that leads you to lasting change.

Integration is a dance—a delicate balance of effort and ease. Some steps will feel natural, while others will challenge you. But with each step, you come closer to embodying the most authentic version of yourself.

This level is an invitation to fully honor your transformation. Savor the process of becoming, instead of feeling like you need to rush to the finish line. Integration is an act of change where you become your highest, most authentic self, an opportunity to embody the life you are creating.

Together, we'll explore how to turn the lessons you've learned into daily practices that anchor you in your higher alignment. You'll discover how to take small, intentional actions that add up to massive transformation. *You don't need to be perfect, but you do need to be present.* Don't worry about how quickly you implement what you've learned—focus on how deeply you can live it.

As you move through this level, remember that you are exactly where you need to be. The work you are doing is life changing, especially when it feels messy or slow. Trust that every moment of alignment, no matter how small, is bringing you closer to the life you envision.

You have everything you need within you.

Integration doesn't ask you to become someone else; it asks you to uncover the truth of who you already are. So, take a deep breath, and let's step into this next phase together. You're not just learning to live differently—you're learning to live fully, as the vibrant, authentic, beautiful soul you were always meant to be . . . and already are deep down.

It's time to learn to *integrate*.

You've got this. Keep going.

CHAPTER 9

FIND YOUR PRACTICE

Transformation isn't a single, life-altering event—it's a series of choices made moment to moment, day by day. It's easy to feel inspired in breakthrough moments when clarity pours in and everything feels possible. But the truth is, transformation takes root in the mundane, in the rhythm of daily life, where inspiration fades and discipline steps forward. This is where our practice becomes essential.

Transformation is like a fire. There's an initial spark—an aha moment, an awakening—that lights the flame, but without tending the fire, even the brightest flame will flicker and die. Practice is what sustains the fire of transformation. It's the fuel that keeps the fire going, steady, and growing. Without practice, the growth you experience can feel fleeting, like a dream slipping through your fingers. But with practice, your transformation becomes tangible—something you live, breathe, and embody.

Your practice matters because it creates consistency in your connection to your higher self. It's one thing to glimpse your potential, but it's another to anchor yourself in it and make it the foundation of how you show up in the world. Your practice is the bridge between who you were and who you're becoming. It's your commitment to your own evolution—a daily act of devotion honoring the bargains you've made with yourself and with Source for this lived experience.

STRENGTHENING THE CONNECTION TO YOUR HIGHER SELF

When you commit to a practice, you're building a relationship with your higher self. This relationship isn't built overnight, and it isn't only sustained when things are easy. Like any meaningful relationship, it requires effort, patience, and showing up, even when you don't feel like it.

Each time you engage in your practice—whether it's meditation, journaling, mindful movement, or sitting in stillness—you're strengthening that connection. You're creating space to hear the whisper of your intuition, the gentle nudge of your inner wisdom. Over time, these whispers grow louder, clearer, and more aligned with the life you are creating.

But practice isn't just about connection; it's also about embodiment. It's one thing to understand a concept intellectually—to know, for example, that forgiveness heals. It's another thing entirely to sit with the discomfort of resentment, to breathe through it, and to actively choose forgiveness in your heart. *Practice makes this possible.* It gives you the tools, the space, and the resilience to align your actions with your highest intentions, even when it's really difficult to do so.

The bargains you've made on this journey—whether with yourself, the universe, or Source—are sacred.

They represent the moments you chose growth over fear, love over limitation, and Faith over doubt. Your practice is how you honor those choices.

Imagine promising your best friend that you'll be there for them, but you never show up. Over time, trust erodes. The same is true for the promises you make to yourself. Without consistent effort, those promises lose their power. But when you show up for your practice, you're sending a clear message to yourself and to the universe: *I am committed to this path. I am choosing alignment. I am choosing me.*

Honoring your promises through practice doesn't mean being perfect. It doesn't mean meditating for an hour every day or flawlessly implementing every tool you've ever learned. It means showing up in whatever way you can, with whatever you have, and doing so with intention. Some days, your practice might look like a deep, soul-connecting meditation. Other days, it might be a quiet moment of gratitude before bed. Both are valid. Both matter.

When you commit to your practice, you're not just changing your own life—you're creating energy that moves far beyond you.

Your alignment, your energy, and your growth have a way of influencing the people around you, often in ways you may not see or realize. Think about the times someone else's calm presence or kind word shifted your entire day. That didn't happen by accident—it happened because they were rooted in their own practice. The same is true for you. When you prioritize your practice, you become a beacon for others, showing what's possible and reminding them of their own capacity for growth.

This energetic effect isn't limited to your immediate circle of friends, family, and acquaintances. As you align more deeply with your soul, you contribute to the awareness of the collective consciousness as well. Your transformation becomes a part of something greater—a rising tide that lifts not only you but also the world around you.

It's important to acknowledge that practice isn't always easy.

There will be days when resistance shows up—when the thought of meditating feels unbearable or when self-doubt whispers that your efforts don't matter. You're not failing in these moments. These moments are invitations to deepen your commitment.

Resistance is often a sign that you're approaching something meaningful. It's the ego's way of clinging to the familiar, even when the familiar no longer serves you. When resistance arises, meet it with compassion. Instead of forcing yourself to push through, pause and ask: What do I need in this moment? Sometimes, the answer will be rest. Other times, it will be to lean in, gently but firmly, and show yourself that you can move through the discomfort anyway.

Your practice doesn't have to be perfect, but you do need to be persistent. Choose to show up, not because it's easy but because you know your growth is worth it.

Your practice is an act of devotion—to your soul, to the life you are creating and to the authentic truth of who you are.

Your practice is a daily choice to align with your highest intentions, even when it feels difficult or inconvenient. This commitment doesn't require grandiose acts because often, it's the smallest, most consistent actions that create the greatest change. A few moments of mindfulness in the morning. A single, conscious breath when stress begins to creep in. A quiet moment of gratitude before you sleep. These acts may seem small, but over time, they build an unshakable foundation that supports your transformation.

Practice matters because it reminds you, every day, of what you're working toward and why it's worth it. It keeps you anchored in truth, even when life feels overwhelming. And it strengthens your connection to the infinite source of wisdom, love, and power within you.

As you move through this chapter, know that your practice is uniquely yours. It doesn't have to look like anyone else's, and it doesn't have to be perfect. It simply has to be intentional.

Take a moment to reflect: What does practice mean to you? How can you begin to create a practice that feels aligned, sustainable, and supportive of your growth? Trust that the answers are already within you, waiting to be uncovered.

You are capable of incredible transformation, and your practice is the key to unlocking it. So, take that first step, however small it may feel, and let it guide you closer to the life—and the self—you've always been destined to embody. You've come this far—you have everything you need to continue.

ELEMENTS OF A PERSONAL PRACTICE

Creating a personal practice is one of the most intimate and transformative gifts you can give to yourself. It's not just a routine or a set of tasks to check off your to-do list—it's a sacred space you carve out to meet yourself as you are, to nurture the parts of you that yearn for growth, and to honor the deep, unspoken truth—you're worthy of this journey.

Building a practice doesn't require perfection, nor does it demand that you get everything right from the start. It only asks that you begin. That you take a step, however small, toward yourself. At its heart, a personal practice is an act of self-love—a declaration that no matter how chaotic or uncertain life may feel, you're committed to your own healing and transformation.

A meaningful practice rests on three pillars: *mindset, consistency, and adaptability.* These are not rules to follow but guiding principles to anchor you. Together, they form the foundation of integration, helping you not only experience change but also live it—breathe it—until it becomes a part of who you are.

Your mindset is the fertile ground where your practice grows.

Without a nurturing mindset, even the most carefully planned efforts can feel heavy and uninviting. The right mindset doesn't mean you have all the answers or start feeling inspired every day. It means you approach your practice with curiosity, patience, and dedication—qualities that gently guide you back to yourself.

Curiosity opens the door to possibility. It whispers to you in moments of doubt, asking, "What if this is exactly where I'm meant to be?" It invites you to explore your practice not as a test to pass but as a journey to embrace. With curiosity, every breath, every stumble, every pause becomes an opportunity to learn. It's through this lens that you discover the beauty of small moments—the quiet clarity of a single inhale, the surprising insight hidden in a seemingly ordinary act.

Patience reminds you that transformation doesn't come in bursts of brilliance but in the steady rhythm of showing up. It's the soft voice that reassures you on the days when your practice feels messy or incomplete: *It's okay. You're still moving forward.* Patience asks that you honor the process, trusting each step is part of a greater unfolding.

Dedication is the quiet promise you make to yourself—a vow to keep showing up, even when you really don't feel like you want to. Dedication celebrates effort. It's the part of you that says, "I'm doing this because I matter. Because my healing, my growth, my joy are worth it to me."

When you nurture a mindset grounded in curiosity, patience, and dedication, your practice becomes a sanctuary. It's no longer about achieving a specific result or meeting external expectations. It's about giving yourself permission to *be*—to rest in the knowledge that you are enough, exactly as you are.

If mindset is the foundation, consistency is the heartbeat of your practice.

It's the quiet rhythm that reminds you to keep going, even when progress feels invisible. But let's be honest—consistency isn't always easy. Life has a way of pulling us in a thousand different directions, and it's tempting to think that if you can't commit fully, it's not worth committing at all.

If you take one thing from this: Know that small steps matter. In fact, they're everything. Transformation doesn't come from a handful of grandiose acts or perfectly executed routines. It comes from the little moments—the five minutes of stillness before bed, the single affirmation spoken in the mirror, the deep breath you take when the world feels overwhelming.

Think of consistency as a series of tiny seeds. Each action you take, no matter how small, plants one. At first, the ground may seem barren, and you may wonder if anything will ever grow at all. But with time, those seeds sprout. Roots take hold. Growth begins. What was once invisible beneath the surface blossoms into something extraordinary.

Consistency doesn't require that you show up perfectly every day—it only asks that you show up as you are. Some days, your practice may feel effortless, like a natural extension of your being. Other days, it may feel like a struggle, a choice you have to make again and again. Both experiences are valid. Both are valuable. What matters is that you keep choosing yourself, that you keep showing up.

As you grow, so will your needs. Allow yourself to adapt.

What serves you today may not serve you tomorrow, and that's not a sign something is wrong—it's a sign of progress. A transformative practice is not rigid; it's alive. It breathes with you, shifts with you, evolves with you. Adaptability is what allows your practice to remain relevant and nourishing, even as life changes.

Adaptability starts with listening—really listening—to yourself. It's about honoring what feels aligned and releasing what doesn't. Maybe your meditation practice expands into journaling or your morning affirmations become a nightly ritual instead. Maybe you swap a high-energy workout for a gentle walk when your body craves rest. Adaptability is the art of meeting yourself where you are with compassion and honesty.

It also means embracing the seasons of your life. There will be times when your practice feels vibrant and expansive, and there will be times when it feels quiet and still. Both are necessary. Both are sacred. Adaptability teaches you to trust the ebb and flow of your journey, to let your practice be a reflection of your life rather than a fixed routine you must adhere to.

When you allow your practice to evolve, you create space for integration. You're no longer trying to fit yourself into a mold or force a structure that no longer resonates. Instead, you're weaving your practice into the fabric of your life, letting it support you in a way that feels natural and sustainable.

When mindset, consistency, and adaptability come together, something beautiful happens: your practice stops feeling like "work" and starts feeling like you.

It becomes a part of your identity, a reflection of your values, a source of strength and joy.

Integration doesn't mean you need to do more. You become more present, and you let your practice move into every aspect of your life—not as a to-do list item to check off but as a gift to yourself. The calm you cultivate in meditation carries into your conversations. The self-compassion you practice during challenging moments extends to how you treat yourself and others. The awareness you develop becomes a guiding light in the dark, helping you navigate life with ease and intention.

This is the essence of a personal practice: It transforms not only how you move through the world but how you *experience* it. It teaches you that growth is not a destination but a way of being, that healing is not about fixing what's broken but embracing what's whole. And that the journey, with all its ups and downs, is what makes you beautifully, authentically, unapologetically *you*.

So, start where you are. Begin with what you have. Trust that every step you take is enough. Your practice is waiting for you—not to change who you are but to help you remember all that you've always been.

BUILDING YOUR PRACTICE

Imagine building a sacred space within yourself—a place you can return to for comfort, clarity, and strength. This is what designing your personal practice offers. It's not just a routine or a checklist; it's a living, breathing reflection of your soul's needs. When you create a practice that feels aligned, it becomes your sanctuary, a place where transformation happens and where you reconnect with the essence of who you are.

This process is deeply personal. It asks you to turn inward, to listen and to honor what feels right for you. There's no blueprint, no right or wrong way to do this. It's about discovering what resonates with you at your core—what moves you, what quiets the noise, what makes you feel whole.

Take a moment to reflect. *What practices light you up?* Maybe you've felt peace in the stillness of meditation or clarity in the pages of a journal. Perhaps you've found freedom in movement or grounding in the rhythm of your breath. Wherever you've felt most connected, that's your starting point. Let it guide you.

Building your practice is never about perfect choices; it's about presence. And step by step, you'll find that your practice becomes a mirror of your growth—a sacred ritual that reminds you of your power, your resilience, and your infinite potential.

Step 1: Start with Intention

Before you begin, ask yourself: Why am I doing this? What is calling me to create this space for myself? Your intention is the heart of your practice. It's what makes it meaningful. Without it, the actions can feel empty, like going through the motions without truly connecting. But when you root your practice in intention, every moment feels purposeful, sacred.

Your intention might be simple but powerful. Perhaps you're seeking stillness in a life that feels chaotic. Or maybe you're looking for healing, clarity, and a deeper connection with your higher self. Whatever it is, hold it close. Let it guide your actions and shape your practice.

Write your intention down as a promise to yourself. Say it aloud as a declaration of your worth. Carry it with you, not just when your practice feels easy but especially when it feels hard. This intention is your anchor. It will keep you grounded and remind you why you started on this path in the first place.

Step 2: Identify a Focus

Life can sometimes feel overwhelming—so many things pulling at your attention, so many areas you want to grow in. But creating a meaningful practice requires focus. It's about choosing one area of your life that feels most aligned with where you are right now.

Ask yourself: What do I need the most in this moment? Maybe it's balance, because you've been giving too much of yourself to others. Maybe it's self-compassion, because the voice in your head has been too critical for too long. Or perhaps it's courage, because you're standing on the edge of something new and uncertain.

There's no rush to get it perfect. Trust your intuition. The area that feels most urgent or sensitive to you right now is where your energy needs to flow. And as you grow, your focus will naturally evolve. Be willing to listen and adapt.

Remember, this is about you. It's not about what you think you *should* focus on but about what you *know* deep down you need the most.

Step 3: Choose Your Tools

Now comes the part where your practice begins to take shape. The tools you choose are what bring your intention to life. Think of them as the ingredients in a recipe—each one adding its own flavor, texture, and nourishment to your experience.

What speaks to you? *Is it the stillness of meditation or the release of journaling? Do you feel called to breathe deeply, move your body, or connect with nature?* Let your intuition guide you toward the practices that feel most natural, most alive.

Start small. You don't need to master a dozen techniques or commit to hours of rituals each day. In fact, simplicity is often where the deepest transformations begin. Choose one or two practices that excite you or bring a sense of peace.

And I want you to know this: It's okay to try something and realize it's not for you. It's okay to change your mind and evolve your tools as you learn more about yourself. There's freedom in this process. It's not about following a rigid plan but about honoring what feels right for you.

Step 4: Create Structure

Structure gives your practice a foundation to stand on. It turns intention into action and ensures your practice becomes a consistent part of your life. But structure doesn't mean rigidity—it's creating a rhythm with your practice that feels supportive, not suffocating.

Start small. Maybe it's five minutes in the morning to breathe, stretch, and set your intention for the day. Maybe it's journaling three times a week or meditating every evening before bed. The key is to set realistic goals that fit into your life as it is now.

Ask yourself: When am I most likely to show up for myself? Is it in the morning, before the world starts pulling you in different directions? Or is it in the stillness of the evening, when the day is done and you can reflect?

Life will happen. There will be days when you miss your practice, and that's okay. What matters is your willingness to return—to show up again and again because you are worth it.

Your practice is not just something you do. It's a relationship—with yourself, with your growth, and with the unseen forces that guide you.

It's a sacred container where you can be fully you, without judgment or expectation. There will be days when your practice feels like coming home—a moment of peace in the chaos. And there will be days when it feels hard, when your mind resists, when showing up feels like the last thing you want to do. Both are part of the journey.

In those challenging moments, remember why you started. Remember your intention, your focus, your *why.* Remember that every time you show up for yourself, you're rewriting the story of your life. You're saying, "I am worth the time. I am worth the effort. I can do this."

Celebrate your practice, no matter how imperfect it may feel. Every breath you take with intention, every word you write, every moment you give to yourself is a victory. It's a declaration that you're committed to your journey and to becoming the fullest expression of who you are.

This is your practice. Yours to create, to nurture, to cherish. Let it be a reflection of your soul and a source of strength, joy, and healing in your life.

Your personal practice is a sacred space where transformation takes root, but it's the tools and practices you integrate into your daily life that bring this space alive.

These are the rituals that nurture your connection to yourself, your authentic self, and the energy of Source. Each practice is an invitation to slow down, to be present, and to align with the energies of growth, healing, and love.

Let's explore some of the tools that can be woven into your daily practice. These tools are not one-size-fits-all; they're a starting point for you to discover what resonates most deeply with who you are.

How you begin and end your day can set the tone for everything in between.

Morning rituals allow you to step into the day grounded and intentional, while evening rituals help you release, reflect, and reconnect.

> Start your morning by creating space for stillness before the demands of the day take over. You might light a candle, set an intention, or simply sit quietly with your breath. Even five minutes of conscious presence can make a big difference. Ask yourself: How do I want to show up today? What energy do I want to carry with me?

In the evening, reflect on the day's events with compassion. Let go of what no longer serves you and celebrate even the smallest victories. Journaling can be a powerful part of this ritual, offering you a moment to process emotions and realign with your purpose. You might also practice gratitude or meditate to clear your mind and prepare for sleep.

Rituals like these don't have to be elaborate; they just need to feel meaningful to you. Let them become the bookends that frame your day with intention and care.

Gratitude is a potent tool for shifting your perspective and raising your vibration.

When you take time to acknowledge the blessings in your life, you train your mind to look for abundance rather than lack, for Faith rather than fear.

Set aside a few minutes each day to write down three to five things you're grateful for. These can be big or small—anything from a kind word from a friend to the warmth of the sun on your face. The act of writing these things down helps us anchor these moments into our consciousness.

For deeper reflection, consider exploring why you're grateful for each item. *For example, if you're thankful for a* peaceful morning, ask yourself what it brought you—calmness, clarity, a *sense of connection?* This practice not only amplifies the feeling of gratitude but also helps you recognize the ways life is supporting you, even when it's subtle.

Over time, you'll find this practice creates a foundation of love and abundance that carries you through life's challenges. It becomes a reminder that, no matter what, there's always something to be thankful for.

Your breath is one of the most powerful tools you have for calming the mind, grounding the body, and connecting with the divine.

When you breathe with intention, you activate the parasympathetic nervous system, signaling to your body that it's safe to relax. This opens the door for deeper states of awareness and connection.

Begin with something simple, like box breathing: inhale for seven counts, hold for seven counts, exhale for seven counts, and hold again for seven counts. Repeat this cycle a few times, noticing how your body begins to settle.

Meditation pairs beautifully with breath work. It doesn't need to be complicated. *Start with just a few minutes of sitting quietly and focusing on your breath. If your mind wanders, gently bring it back to the present moment without judgment.*

For those seeking a deeper connection with Source, visualization meditations can be especially powerful. *Imagine a beam of light flowing through your body, cleansing and energizing every cell. Or picture yourself surrounded by an infinite presence of love, feeling supported and guided.* These practices are not about achieving perfection or silencing the mind. They're about showing up, even when it feels messy, and trusting that the effort is enough.

Your imagination is a bridge between the present and the future.

When you visualize the highest version of yourself, you begin to align your energy with that reality, making it easier to manifest your desires.

Find a quiet space where you won't be disturbed. Close your eyes and take a few deep breaths to center yourself. Then, imagine your highest self—the version of you that is confident, loving, and aligned. What do they look like? How do they carry themselves? What does their energy feel like?

Step into their shoes. See the world through their eyes. Visualize yourself moving through your day as this version of you, making decisions, interacting with others, and creating with intention. Feel the emotions that come with embodying this energy—joy, gratitude, peace, love.

The more vividly you can imagine this version of yourself, the more you begin to embody their traits in your daily life. Visualization is not just a mental exercise; it's an energetic one, a way to align your vibration with your aspirations.

Your body is a vessel for your spirit, and moving it with intention can help you release stagnant energy, reconnect with your energy, and feel more aligned.

Yoga is a beautiful practice for bringing the body and spirit into alignment. Its combination of mindful movement, breath, and presence creates a space for healing and transformation. Whether you're a seasoned yogi or a complete beginner, you can find a style that resonates with you.

If yoga isn't your thing, consider walking in nature. Feel the earth beneath your feet, the breeze on your skin, and the rhythm of your breath as you move. Nature has a grounding energy that reminds you of your connection to something greater.

Dance is another powerful form of movement. Let go of any judgment and allow your body to move freely to the music. Dance can be a form of release, a way to express emotions that words cannot capture.

Whatever practice you choose, let it be a celebration of your body and spirit. Move in a way that feels joyful, intuitive, and loving.

INTEGRATING PRACTICES INTO YOUR LIFE

The beauty of these tools is that they are adaptable—you can mix, match, and modify them to fit your needs. Start small, experiment, and notice what feels most supportive. Over time, these practices will weave themselves into the fabric of your life, becoming a source of strength, clarity, and connection.

Remember, the goal is to show up with intention. Trust that even the smallest effort has the power to create profound shifts in your life. Each breath, each step, each moment of presence is a gift you give yourself—a reminder of your worth and your infinite potential.

Our journey of transformation is not without its challenges. Even with the best intentions, life often presents obstacles that make consistency feel like an uphill battle. Time constraints, self-doubt, resistance, and even fear of change can arise, threatening to derail our efforts. But remember that these challenges are part of the process—they're opportunities to grow stronger, to reaffirm your commitment and to deepen your practice.

Let's explore some of the most common obstacles and the strategies that can help you overcome them, allowing your personal practice to thrive.

One of the most common challenges is finding the time to integrate daily practices into an already packed schedule.

When life feels chaotic, it's easy to let your rituals slip, convincing yourself that you'll get back to them "when things settle down." But the truth is, life rarely slows down on its own—it's up to you to create space for what matters.

Start by reframing your perspective: *Your personal practice is not another task on your to-do list.* It's the foundation that supports everything else in your life. Even five minutes can make a difference. For example, a short morning ritual or a quick journaling session in the evening can help you feel grounded and focused, no matter how busy your day may be.

If carving out time feels impossible, consider integrating your practices into your existing routines. Practice breath work during your commute, reflect on what you're grateful for while brushing your teeth, and take mindful breaths before each meal. These micro moments may seem small, but over time, they accumulate into meaningful progress.

Self-doubt is a quiet but persistent companion as we transform.

You might question whether you're "doing it right" or if your efforts are even making a difference. This inner critic thrives on perfectionism, creating a narrative that you're not enough or that you'll never succeed.

The antidote to self-doubt is trust—*in the process, in your ability to grow, and in the timing of your life.* It's important to remember that change isn't linear; it's a winding path with peaks and valleys. Progress might not always be visible, but every step, no matter how small, contributes to your evolution.

To quiet self-doubt, try reflecting on your "why." *Why did you begin this journey? What drew you to these practices?* Connecting with your purpose can reignite your motivation and remind you that the journey is worthwhile, even when doubts arise.

Resistance often shows up when we're about to step into something new.

It's the mind's way of protecting us from the unknown, clinging to the familiar even if it no longer serves us. Resistance can manifest as procrastination, avoidance, or even physical discomfort when engaging in your practice.

The key to overcoming resistance is awareness. When you notice it creeping in, pause and ask yourself: *What am I afraid of?* Resistance is the shadow we know as fear—of failure, of success, and of change itself. By naming the fear, you take away some of its power and create space for action.

Take small, manageable steps to move through resistance. If sitting for a 20-minute meditation feels overwhelming, start with two. If journaling feels daunting, write a single sentence. Action, no matter how small, helps dissolve resistance and builds momentum over time.

Consistency is required for meaningful growth, but it doesn't require daily perfection in your practice.

In fact, it's the imperfect, messy moments that teach us the most about ourselves. Let's go over a few strategies to help you stay consistent with your practice.

Focus on progress, not perfection.

Perfectionism can paralyze you, convincing you that if you can't do something perfectly, it's not worth doing at all. But the truth is, elevating into a higher version of yourself isn't about being perfect; it's about showing up, even when it's messy, when you aren't sure you know what you're doing.

Allow yourself to be human. Missed a morning ritual? No problem—start fresh in the evening. Struggled to stay focused during meditation? That's okay—acknowledge it and try again tomorrow. Every effort is a step on your path. Celebrate your progress, every step you take, reflecting on where you started and the shifts you've experienced along the way.

Develop compassion for yourself.

Setbacks are inevitable, but they're not obstacles. They're opportunities to learn, to practice self-compassion, and to recommit to your journey. How you respond is far more important than the setback itself.

When you stumble, resist the urge to beat yourself up. Instead, treat yourself with the same kindness and understanding you would offer someone you love. Ask yourself: What can I learn from this moment? How can I support myself as I move forward?

Self-compassion isn't excusing bad behavior or lowering your standards—it's about creating a safe space for your growth. When you approach yourself with kindness, you build strength, making it easier to move through life's challenges.

Embrace the journey of remembering who you are.

Overcoming challenges in our practice doesn't mean we eliminate obstacles—we learn how to navigate them with Grace. Each time we face resistance, self-doubt, and time constraints, we have an opportunity to deepen our commitment and grow stronger in the process.

This journey is uniquely yours. There's no right or wrong way to move forward—there's only the way that feels authentic and sustainable for you. Trust that every effort you make is guiding you closer to the life you envision.

Be patient with yourself. Transformation takes time, and the path isn't linear. Celebrate your victories, learn from your setbacks, and keep showing up. Each day is an opportunity to reconnect with your purpose, your practice, and your infinite potential.

Every choice you make sends out energy through the fabric of life.

Whether you're aware of it or not, the way you live, heal, and grow doesn't just shape your personal journey—it touches the lives of others and contributes to the collective energy of the world. Your individual practices are not just acts of self-transformation; they are threads woven into humanity's shared evolution.

When we dedicate ourselves to healing and growth, we become part of something much greater than ourselves.

Each time we release an old wound, let go of limiting beliefs, or reconnect with our higher self, we contribute to the healing of the collective consciousness.

Imagine the light of a single candle igniting in a dark room. That light becomes a beacon—spreading, illuminating not just your path but the paths of those around you. When you do the work to heal, you create space for others to step into their own healing. Your energy shifts, and without saying a word, you send a message to those around you: *If I'm capable of transformation, so are you.*

This isn't an abstract idea; it's something we see in the small, everyday choices we make. When we choose love over lack, compassion over judgment, and alignment over chaos, we send this energy outward.

This movement of energy has the power to uplift not just those closest to you but the collective awareness as a whole. Your personal transformation sparks collective healing.

Living in alignment with your authentic self is a quiet but powerful act of leadership.

When you show up authentically and stay true to who you are, you inspire others to reflect on their own lives. People notice when you respond to life's challenges with Grace. They notice when you choose to prioritize self-care and speak from a place of integrity.

Inspiration doesn't come from preaching or persuading; it comes from simply being. Your actions, not your words, carry the most profound impact. Someone in your circle may see you stepping boldly into your truth and feel the nudge to do the same. A friend might observe the consistency of your practice and feel encouraged to begin their own. Even strangers can sense the energy you bring into a space.

Think of it like dropping a stone into a still lake. The waves may start small, but they expand outward, touching every corner of the water. When you choose alignment, you don't just transform your own experience—you influence the collective in ways you may never fully see or understand.

Be the first spark.

Stepping into your practice often requires courage, especially when it means walking a path others might not yet understand. But the fire of awakening starts with a single spark. When we embrace our healing, growth, and authenticity, we become the very spark that sets change in motion.

Our courage gives others permission to explore their own potential. When they see us navigating our challenges, rising after setbacks, and continuing forward with Grace, it plants a seed of possibility in their hearts. We don't need everything figured out to inspire others; our willingness to show up, even imperfectly, is enough.

Over time, these energetic waves of individual transformation create a collective wave. What starts as a personal journey becomes part of a larger movement, awakening and empowering more and more people to align with their soul's calling.

The wave effect of energy is a beautiful reflection of how deeply connected we all are. Though it can feel like we're navigating life alone, we're all threads in the same web, woven together in ways seen and unseen.

Your energy is never isolated—it interacts, influences, and intertwines with the world around you.

When you rise, you help lift others. When you heal, you make it possible for others to heal. And as you align with your truest self, you create an energy that moves outward into families, communities, and even generations to come.

This is the sacred act of transformation: As you grow, you inspire others to rise alongside you. And as they grow, they pull you even higher.

Keep showing up. Commit to your growth, even when it feels difficult or uncertain. Together, we are building a foundation for a better world—a world where individual healing is the spark for collective transformation.

Take messy action.

Every time you show up for yourself, no matter how imperfect the action feels, you're choosing love—for who you are now and for who you are becoming. In a world that's constantly distracting us, choosing to pause and connect with your practice is a revolutionary act. It's a bold statement that you're worthy of healing, worthy of growth, and worthy of living a life that feels aligned with your soul's deepest truths.

Your practice is about finding the courage to meet yourself where you are, even in the messiest of moments. When the weight of resistance feels unbearable, when doubt creeps in and tells you to quit, remember: Every breath, every small action, every intention to try again is a testament to your strength. You are rewriting your story with every step forward, no matter how shaky it feels.

This journey was never meant to be neat and tidy. It's in the rawness of the process—the stumbles, the breakthroughs, and the quiet moments of clarity—that we transform. Every time you rise, even when it feels like you can't, you send a powerful message to Source: *I am here. I am healing. I am becoming. I am remembering who I am.*

You may not see it yet, but you're making a difference. Your choice to heal is a light in the darkness, a spark that ignites hope in others. Your courage to grow inspires those around you to look within themselves. And your unwavering commitment to alignment isn't just for you—it's for all of us.

So, when it feels hard, remember you're not walking this path alone. Each step you take is supported by the energy of those who have walked before you and those rising alongside you now. Together, we're weaving a web of transformation—one choice, one action, one moment of self-love at a time.

You are stronger than you realize, more capable than you know, and always exactly where you need to be. The world needs your light. Trust the process. Trust yourself. And trust that every step you take brings you closer to a life that feels whole and free.

You've got this. Keep going.

CHAPTER 10

OUR AGREEMENTS WITH SOURCE

Becoming who we're meant to be—overflowing with self-love, connected to what lights us up, and stepping into the purpose we came here for—requires us to honor a set of agreements with Source. These aren't rules we're forced to follow but promises we made before we even got here. They're the compass that guides you through the mess, the magic, and everything in between.

These agreements form the foundation for everything you want to build. Without them, self-love has nowhere to land, and the expanded awareness you're seeking feels shaky at best. But when you lean in to them, they give you something solid—a structure that allows you to rise higher, dream bigger, and create a life that feels aligned with your soul.

Sometimes, though, awakening shows us a hard truth: The foundation we've been standing on wasn't built to last. We realize we've been balancing on something fragile, something that can't support the weight of who we're becoming. And as painful as it is, we often have to let it fall apart. The beliefs, the patterns, the identities we once clung to—they all have to crumble so we can rebuild on something real.

Breaking ourselves down isn't easy. It's raw. It's vulnerable. But it's also the most courageous thing you'll ever do. Because in that process, you're not just tearing apart what no longer serves you—you're making space for the truth of who you are. And that's where the magic happens.

These agreements, these promises you made with Source, are the same for all of us. They're unshakable, eternal, and woven into the fabric of who we are. But the way we meet them? That's an individual process. Each of us has our own path to walk, our own lessons to learn, and our own foundation to rebuild. And even though it looks different for everyone, the truth remains: When we honor these promises, everything shifts.

Doors that felt locked suddenly swing open. What once seemed out of reach becomes possible. Life starts to feel less like something we're surviving and more like something we're co-creating. Honoring these agreements helps us find balance—between light and dark, giving and receiving, surrender and action. It's not always easy, but it is worth it. Because on the other side of the work is a life that feels expansive and free. A life where the beauty of this world shines a little brighter, where you feel more at home in yourself, and where you start to remember: This is what you came here for.

You're stronger than you think. Every step you take, even the wobbly ones, is rebuilding a foundation that can hold the fullness of who you are. Trust in the process. Trust in yourself. And trust that every promise you honor brings you closer to the life your soul has been waiting for.

The world becomes so beautiful and open when you do.

TAKE CARE OF YOUR BODY

Your body is something you need to learn to love, something you need to learn to take proper care of. The body is a complex organism designed to do amazing things if we allow it to.

The body isn't who we are, but it is an external representation of our soul, our struggles, and the energy we're processing or refusing to look at. Just as your soul came here to learn and to grow with emotional experiences, learning to operate the human body you're in is equally as important.

Many of us come into this world inheriting generational trauma and limiting beliefs about our bodies. Both of these deeply affect the function and health of the body. When you embody the truth that you are a soul operating within a human body, that's when the relationship to your body changes.

Our agreement with Source stated we would learn how to operate our human body to the best of our ability, and in doing so the human body will be the vehicle with which we accomplish the missions and purposes we're here to fulfill—both learning and growing together.

This is the operating manual for the human body—the things you need to do to ensure it's functioning at its best. Most of these things sound simple, because they are. Reprogramming limiting beliefs and sticking to your care schedule, when your environment encourages you to do otherwise, is what makes things difficult.

Rise to the challenge and integrate the practice of caring for your body.

Here's how:

- **Say nice things to yourself.** Poor self-talk makes the human body pretty miserable. It has systems in place to find in the physical what you're creating in your head. The more negative you are, the more your body builds an environment of inflammation, leading to disease. Speak to yourself the way you would your best friend, a child, a pet, or really anyone you care deeply for. Shifting your mind out of negative thought patterns takes time and effort. Be relentless. Do the work. It will become a habit. Speaking kindly to yourself will become your default way of thinking if you stick with it. Making the switch is the most energy-intensive part. Being nice becomes easy once you leave the old habits behind.
- **Sleep.** Your body needs you to check out of the active three-dimensional experience everyday so it can run its rest and repair programs while you sleep. Stop staying up too late. Put your phone down and turn the television off. Stop falling asleep with the television on. You're programming your subconscious when you do that. Use

white noise simulators if you need help falling asleep. Avoid using substances to help you sleep. It's better to have several difficult nights training the body how to fall asleep quickly than to rely on substances that put you into a version of sleep that doesn't do the rest and repair work that's needed. The quality of your sleep matters. Deep sleep allows your body to heal. It's common for the body to need extra sleep in the early stages of healing. Allow yourself to take the time you need to rest. Sometimes we feel great with less and sometimes we need a lot more. Honor what you need.

- **Meditate daily.** Source wants to check in with you, and you operate at your best when your mind and nervous system are calm and regulated. Meditation allows you cut through the noise of the world. It allows you to center yourself and feel the connection with the Creator you have access to if you would simply quiet the mind. Meditation isn't just the time you spend fully tapped in, experiencing the quantum realm but also how you move through the world. Meditation is an act of presence. Being present in the moments of your life is also an act of meditation—an act of connection with Source so that you may co-create the life you are living. In the beginning of the healing process, longer, deeper meditations are required for the reprogramming and healing of your mind and body. As you progress you may find other ways to find the present moment through your day, places where you find flow and focus. Embrace the additional places and spaces to center throughout your day while maintaining a foundational practice.
- **Eat intuitively.** There's no perfect diet. There's no magical formula. I spent decades looking for it just to find out we need to eat what makes us feel our best, while understanding what we think and how we feel about the foods we consume changes how we digest them. When you believe a food is bad, your body hears you.

When you believe a food is good, your body hears you. Eating intuitively can be simple. Eat whole foods that agree with your body. Limit food with a lot of additives, food coloring, and preservatives as often as you can. Eat when your body is hungry, and stop when your body is full. Eating, just like everything else, is about balance. Experience delicious food while learning the balance of how much is too much. Understanding what the body you're in needs is part of the adventure of life. Be excited that you get to learn what you need. Pay attention to when you reach for food as a coping mechanism. We can reach for food when we feel ungrounded in our body, to avoid emotions, and to cope with trauma and not feeling safe. Be kind to yourself if you struggle with using food to cope. Using nervous system regulation tools in moments of struggle can help shift the habit to reach for food. Nourish the body. Take care of the vehicle moving you around this world.

- **Move your body intuitively.** Walk, cycle, lift weights, hike, do yoga, take a Pilates class, dance, stretch. Do something. Find movement you enjoy. We need to move our bodies. We feel better when do; the body appreciates movement. Physically moving energy around keeps the body happy and healthy. Find something you like to do and do it. There's no time limit or intensity you have to reach. Take a look at how much you're moving. How would it feel if you did more, or less? Moving your body, just like eating food, is about finding the balance that works for you. We are all different. We require different amounts, different intensities, and what we do and how long we do it for varies throughout our life. While one person may struggle to get off the couch, another will overexercise to the point of injury. Movement includes muscle manipulation, massage, stretching, and foam rolling. Find your balance.

- **Stay hydrated.** The body is made up largely of water. It serves many functions in the body, and drinking enough is like making sure there's oil in your car. Your engine doesn't run right without it. Your body functions will suffer if you aren't drinking enough water. They will also suffer if you drink too much. Find your balance.

These are the agreements you made with Source when you entered the body. Honor them.

MAKE AND MAINTAIN BOUNDARIES

Boundaries are the rules of engagement we set with the world around us. The people, places, and things we engage with during the course of our time here will require boundaries. Boundaries dictate how we move through the world. Part of the mission we chose is remembering what our boundaries are, declaring them, and then enforcing them.

We aren't doing ourselves or anyone else any favors by refusing to set boundaries. Being a people-pleasing doormat is just as harmful for the world around you as it is for you as an individual. The people around you need to understand what the rules of engagement are when they interact with you. Boundaries also give the people you hold dear the opportunity to elevate themselves. Without a boundary, we don't always see how our behavior affects others.

I struggled with learning how to make boundaries. My clients struggle, and I would bet you've found holding boundaries difficult at times too. Remembering the boundaries you need to set—and reinforce—requires healing. It requires understanding and integrating your self-worth. It's a tall order to make until you heal from self-deprecating beliefs.

Limiting beliefs stand between you and the life your soul expects you to live. The higher self knows the boundaries, understands the boundaries, and honors them. The higher self exists in a place and space where healthy boundaries are simply part of the experience. Tap into your higher self. See how worthy you really are.

Remember, you can change the cost of what it takes to access you at any time. Set boundaries. Move toward your higher self—the act of doing so pulls everyone around you up vibrationally. Changing your rules of engagement literally changes the world.

There will be people who do not respect your boundaries. That's okay. It's not your job to force change. It's your job to enforce your boundaries regardless of resistance to them. When you hold your boundaries, you signal to the universe you remember your value. When you remember your value, the universe responds with rewards, new opportunities, and people who respect and value your boundaries, because they have them too.

Holding your boundaries sets the tone for everyone to move along on the highest available path. We are all playing roles in each other's lives. A person who disrespects your boundaries and is removed from your story can play a caring role in someone else's. It's in the act of holding your boundaries that the offending party gets to where they need to go. Rejection is always redirection.

Holding your boundaries ensures everyone gets to play the part they were meant to play. These roles are not bad or good; they are a momentary experience of perspective. Embody yours.

Remember your value. Make and hold your boundaries. They help us all.

GROUND AND CONNECT

Being in nature is how we were originally designed to live. Our bodies thrive in the rhythms, sounds, and vibrations of the natural world. But in modern life, so many of us spend most of our time indoors, disconnected from the earth beneath our feet and the energy it offers. The truth is, Gaia—our living, breathing planet—plays a vital role in helping us stay grounded. Just as our bodies process emotions and energy, the earth processes and transforms energy as well.

Gaia isn't just the ground we walk on; she's an organism, alive in every sense. Her rivers flow like arteries, her forests breathe as lungs, and her energy centers vibrate just like ours. As we evolve spiritually and raise our vibration, Gaia evolves with us. Our connection to her isn't just symbolic; it's an active, reciprocal relationship.

For many of us, that connection has grown weaker over time. Western society often teaches us to see ourselves as separate from nature, rather than part of its intricate web. But we're not separate—we're interwoven with the earth, and our health, happiness, and sense of balance reflect that. When we reconnect with Gaia, something shifts. We feel calmer, more whole, and more in tune with ourselves and the world around us.

Grounding, also known as earthing, is one of the simplest ways to restore that connection. It's the act of physically connecting your body to the earth—standing barefoot on the grass, touching a tree, or even lying on the ground. And it's not just a spiritual practice; the science backs it up. Studies show that grounding can improve sleep, reduce inflammation, balance cortisol levels, enhance blood flow, and support cellular repair. It even boosts endorphins and increases heart rate variability, which is a marker of nervous system resilience.

How it works on an energetic level is the earth's surface is abundant with free electrons. These electrons are like nature's reset button for your body. When you connect with the ground, the earth's electrons flow into your body, neutralizing excess positive charges caused by things like stress, inflammation, and exposure to electronic devices. Think of it as balancing out static electricity—it helps bring your energy system back to equilibrium, leaving you feeling more grounded, calm, and restored.

But grounding isn't just about electrons. Nature speaks to us in subtle ways. The sound of birds singing, for example, sends signals to the brain that we're safe, helping shift us out of fight-or-flight mode into a more calm and relaxed state. It's amazing how something as simple as stepping outside can transform our mental and physical well-being.

Whenever you feel stressed or anxious, try heading outside. Put your feet on the earth or rest your hands against a tree. If it's too cold or the weather isn't cooperating, there are grounding mats, socks, and sheets that allow you to connect indoors using the electrical ground in your homes. Whatever method you choose, grounding clears away stagnant energy and offers it back to Gaia. And here's the beautiful part: Gaia transforms that energy into something beneficial for the planet. It's a perfect exchange—healing for you and nourishment for her.

Take a few deep breaths while you're grounding, and you'll likely feel your stress and tension melt away. Even just a couple of minutes a day makes a difference.

Getting outside also allows you to access the healing powers of the sun. Studies have shown that getting outside first thing in the morning helps regulate hormones, balance your sleep-wake cycle, and boost energy and mood. Plus, sunlight on your skin triggers your body to produce vitamin D, an essential nutrient that most of us don't get enough of. While supplements can help, there's something uniquely nourishing about receiving vitamin D straight from the source.

Grounding and connecting with nature is more than just a practice; it's a way to honor the connection between your mind, body, soul, and the earth. Step outside, breathe deeply, and let Gaia remind you that you're supported. Your entire being will thank you for it.

MISTAKES HAPPEN

I've tripped and fallen on my face more times than I can count in this life. I've even had the experience of getting to face the mistakes I've made in other incarnations. Mistakes are a necessary part of growth—a fact I will shout from the rooftops.

If you have big goals, big dreams, it's important that you expect to fail. Living as your authentic self requires a lot of messy action and choosing the vibration of Faith over fear. Moving on your highest path means failing more times than the person who's too afraid to start. High-vibrational experience requires failing forward.

Having a high-vibrational experience does not necessarily mean you have a giant house, a private jet, and endless vacations . . . although it could. Generally, a high-vibrational life is one where you continually walk toward the highest version of yourself. It's looking at your life and feeling immense gratitude for the connections you've developed with the souls and the world around you. High vibration is feeling your connection to Source. It is joy. It is bliss. It is resilience in the face of a challenge. It's the act of being in the present moment. It's the beauty and awe for everything in and all around you . . . including your mistakes.

You weren't built to be perfect or a carbon copy of someone else. In fact, every last one of us is different. Unique. You are meant to experience the world differently from everyone around you. It's in the originality of you, your authenticity, that Source gets to experience life through your eyes, through your unique experience of the world.

When you entered into the bargain of life with Source, you agreed to come into the world screaming, blank, and completely unaware of who you are and what you agreed to accomplish here. You are meant to learn through your mistakes. You have no other choice. You can't do your best until you learn how to do so.

While failing forward through life can be a tough pill to swallow, all you have to do is take a look at how the toddler version of you experienced life. As a kid, you bumped into life. You decided what you liked through play. No one judged why you liked one stuffed animal over another, and no one questioned why you didn't know your alphabet or how to write your name on the first try. Being an adult is no different. Whoever made you think you needed to have all your steps planned out and everything figured out in advance didn't understand how soul exploration works.

You are meant to learn and grow through your mistakes.

Our agreement with Source is if we fall, we dust ourselves off and get back up. We bargained that we'd be resilient. Failures will have hard and soft landings, and the harder ones create more opportunity for growth. Integrating strength means you have to be strong. Rising requires falling first. Source always provides everything you need for your journey, and you expand exponentially when you settle into the truth that you don't always know what it is you are accomplishing or what order you are doing it in until after it happens. Trust Source and the journey.

If you've fallen, there's always a way to get back up.

When we make mistakes, dense emotions like guilt and shame make themselves known. Mistakes are junction points, places that allow access to multiple timelines. They're spots where what you choose to focus on and how you perceive the experience determines the vibration of what you do next. Guilt and shame are the lowest vibrational resonances, meaning every time guilt and shame show up and you focus on them, creating narratives around those emotions, you slide downward into a lower version of yourself. Prioritize healing the parts of your soul sitting in the shadow of guilt and shame. Transmute that energy and let it leave your life.

We all make mistakes. Some are life altering, and some are small. Regardless of the size of the mistake, focusing on it instead of the lesson provided creates the negative thought patterns and emotions that hold you back. Anxiety disorders are the fixation of the mind on previous and potential mistakes.

Source making the agreement with you, insisting you continue on, learning from your mistakes instead of stressing over them, shows you the path of growth. As you make mistakes and learn, your soul evolves, expanding Source's understanding of the lived experience as much as your own.

Source is unconditional love. There is no judgment, just learning.

Learn to get comfortable in the uncomfortableness of it all. Mistakes are your opportunity to pivot, to grow and to create beauty where you didn't know any could exist.

Make the messes into masterpieces.

DO YOUR BEST WITH GRACE

Operating from the belief that we are all doing our best with the information and knowledge we have allows you to move through your life with the space needed for love and kindness for all.

The people who annoy you, the people you disagree with, and the people who hurt you are moving through life doing the best they can. It may not feel like it in your denser interactions, but it's true. Even when it feels like it's not enough, even when you hurt others out of spite, when others hurt you, when it feels intentional, and when mistakes were clearly made. We're all doing our best.

We can't do better until we know what better is.

Every single soul is doing the best with what they have. It looks different for everyone. Some may have been here many times, having had vast experience in the density of Earth; others have not. Some have alchemized the pain in their lives and lineages; others have not. Many are somewhere in the middle.

Face mistakes with nonjudgment and release any shame you're carrying. You have a better chance at elevating to your best when you do.

When figuring out the most authentic way to show up and live your life, your best will look different every day. We are always ebbing and flowing, learning and growing. This is how you learn what your personal best is.

Doing your best is an agreement you hold with Source and Source alone.

Other people may hold the ability to judge you based on their beliefs and ideals, but your best is not between you and them; it's between you and Source. You know when you are making the highest available choice and when you are not. Source knows too.

It's not your job to focus on anyone's best but your own.

When you focus on doing your best, you learn to unconditionally love your authenticity. You embrace what you are good at and your mistakes. You walk with the frequency of Grace, understanding you do your best in every moment, even when that can look drastically different between the times and spaces in your life.

Focus on doing your best. No one knows what that is but you.

REGULATE YOUR NERVOUS SYSTEM

Regulating your nervous system, even if you don't know how to do anything else, will change your entire life. I should know—it changed mine.

I remember the moment I made the choice to sit through the uncomfortableness of getting my nervous system dialed in. It was before I learned how to access the quantum realm, the in-between spaces, and it was before I understood how important meditating was. It was a random Friday night many years ago. It was a night where I had no plans, and nothing to do, a night where I would've normally found something, anything, to fill the time with—because my nervous system was terrified of sitting still.

It took me a long time to unravel all the reasons why I felt the way I felt. It took me just as long to heal from all of those traumas, triggers, belief structures, and internalized wounds—once I realized what they were. And I wouldn't have been able to do any of it if I didn't just sit in the uncomfortableness of my nervous system that random Friday night so long ago.

Fight-or-flight doesn't look like screaming and subsequently running away most of the time. Having a nervous system stuck in fight-or-flight shows itself as avoidance-style behaviors, hiding in being busy, numbing out with food, over-exercising, binge-watching TV, doom-scrolling, using substances, and spending time with people you don't even like just to fill the time. All these things are just as much a fight-or-flight response from the nervous system as physically running away is. You can be afraid of your emotions just as much as a physical threat. Your nervous system doesn't know the difference, and when you don't know how to face and process your emotions head-on, you'll struggle with inappropriate coping mechanisms to avoid them.

The nervous system controls virtually every cell, organ system, and tissue in the body. An unregulated nervous system will cause havoc with your mental and physical health if left in a misregulated state.

Many of us spend decades in fight-or-flight before we learn how to regulate. That random Friday night, I fought with all I had. You'd think it would be easy to sit in my comfortable apartment, put on a TV show, and spend the night calmly with myself, but my mind started racing almost instantly. My brain went through every option it could muster to get me to walk toward some dopamine and a distraction.

For decades, my nervous system was beat up and berated. It happened internally with ingrained limiting beliefs and unhealthy thought patterns. Externally, I had to leave unhealthy relationships before a safe and calm environment became available to me. I lived with my nervous system on high alert for a really long time. My body didn't know what it was like to move through life without a threat to defend or hide myself from. But that random Friday night, there was no threat. There was just me, my dogs, and a couch I could not sit calmly on because I had never experienced what that was like.

When your nervous system optimizes a chaotic environment to keep you safe, your body does not know what to do with calm. It doesn't know what to do with peace. The nervous system doesn't recognize it. So, even when you want to experience these states of being and they are available, until you learn to regulate the nervous system, you'll end up sabotaging yourself right back into the chaos.

Regulating your nervous system—for the first time—is very much like breaking a horse that hasn't had a rider yet. You feed the horse, you walk the horse, you pet the horse, and the horse loves you. But the horse is used to doing as it pleases without the weight of you on its back, without you controlling it. When you decide to hop on for a ride, the horse rebels. It does everything in its power to throw you off. It kicks, it rears up, it runs around wildly. Breaking a horse requires that you hop on confidently and hold on for dear life. You have to hold your position until the horse submits to your direction and control.

The nervous system is no different. You have to take determined action and hold your position until the nervous system relaxes.

Anticipate the process will be a wild ride initially. It's uncomfortable in the beginning. I can laugh at the fact that it took everything I had to just sit still and avoid unhealthy coping mechanisms now, but it didn't feel funny then. It was physically and mentally exhausting to break those patterns, but I did it. My clients and members do it. You can do it.

The first time we try and succeed provides a hard reset of the nervous system. Holding to that change is an ongoing process. Initially, we use strength and sheer will to tame the nervous system out of unhealthy coping mechanisms. Maintenance requires commitment to the journey.

Making healthy and aligned choices the automatic, easy option for the mind and body means that you'll have to regulate your nervous system daily. You have to ride the proverbial horse, exercise it, and take care of it. A horse without a rider for long enough returns to the wild.

Regulating the nervous system is a nonnegotiable. It is an agreement you made with Source. Not your easiest agreement, by far. Things like constant access to e-mail and text messages, exposing the eyes to artificial light long after the sun has gone down, streams of "breaking" news updates, artificial food, and social media notifications are just a few of the things that can stress out your nervous system.

Getting over the initial things you'll face with the first reset of your nervous system gives way to the vast expanse of daily stressors. This is why regulating the nervous system is a nonnegotiable. Having a flexible nervous system is required for higher vibrational experiences.

Some of the best ways to regulate:

- **Cold therapy:** Cryotherapy, cold plunge tanks, ice packs on the chest and face, going outside in cold temperatures, and cold showers all work.
- **Breath work:** Take a deep inhale, hold for a count of seven, exhale and hold for a count of seven, and repeat for several cycles until you calm down.
- **Ground:** Put your feet to the ground or your hands on a tree; the nervous system is electrical, so go ground out your circuits.
- **Dance:** Movement to music signals to the body it isn't in danger; get your groove on.
- **Shake:** Just like a dog shakes to reset their nervous system, take a move from man's best friend and T. Swift and just shake it off.

In addition to regulation, determine how to give yourself the best environment to thrive. Remove as many stressors as possible. Clean up your external and internal environments—people, places, and things that you know are not for your highest good, let them go. Your nervous system will thank you. This includes substances that agitate the nervous system. Alcohol, marijuana products, an excess of foods that are high in sugar, processed foods, and too much caffeine all stimulate the nervous system.

Be mindful and pay attention to what makes your body feel good and what makes it more difficult for you to regulate your nervous system. Doing so will allow you to create a safe and supportive environment—internally and externally—for yourself.

You can learn to create an environment that makes regulation easy. Support and regulate your nervous system. You won't regret it.

SPEAK YOUR TRUTH

You're not doing anyone any favors by keeping all your thoughts, feelings, and beliefs to yourself. In fact, bottling everything up leads to a lot of physical and mental health problems.

We have an agreement with Source to speak our truth.

Many of us struggle with speaking our truth, and we struggle even more when what we know to be true is different from the general narrative of society and social circles. It's okay to be different. Truth isn't always accepted or understood. Source only asks that you speak your understanding of truth, you're not being asked to convince anyone else.

Truth comes from a deep internal knowing, from a place of light, of unconditional love. It's a place that is not fearful, manipulative, or self-serving. In order to access truth, you must heal. When you speak from trauma, the shadow influences the analytical mind, and you end up declaring your wounds as your truth.

When you heal, you learn to share your experiences while being open to other perspectives. You learn what healthy boundaries are, and you maintain them. When you open yourself up while having healthy boundaries, you create the space to meet your authenticity. You gain an understanding of what's important to you and what you light up for. Speaking your truth requires understanding yourself.

Never silence who you are. When you learn to communicate from your truth, you end up living your highest available experience.

Speak your truth.

EMBRACE AUTHENTICITY

A major struggle you'll overcome when healing is the inability to feel loved as your authentic self. So many of us have an internal narrative that somehow a mistake was made when we were created, and we need to fix everything about us to be worthy of love and acceptance.

We made an agreement with Source to be ourselves—to stand in our authenticity and enjoy it.

The idea that we need to change into something we are not, pursue dreams that are not ours, and somehow fit into the ever-changing ideals society presses upon us, is resistance—resistance you came here to alchemize.

Being authentic requires you to show up in a way that releases the fear of being accepted and understood. You face the fear of rejection head-on. Authenticity says "Here I am. If you like me, great. If you don't, that's okay too because I'm going to be authentically me anyway." The more you embrace your authenticity, the more unconditional love you experience. Because being authentic is a form of unconditional love of self. Being authentic is a mission in and of itself. You are a completely original expression of Source. You were meant to live as such.

It can be hard to fully live in our authenticity. The resistance around us spins the narrative that if we're too authentic, we won't fit in, and if we don't fit in, we'll be left behind and left out of society entirely. *Do it anyway.* That narrative isn't true. You will find the community who supports you when you reject false versions of yourself. The friends and family that truly align with who you are at a soul level show up.

Show up as yourself in spite of fear. Doing so will end up being one of the things you're most proud of.

Comparison is an authenticity killer. If you want to stand in your authenticity, you have to let go of comparison. Comparison is the fastest way to doubt yourself, degrade your own capabilities, and give your energy away, drawing in denser experiences instead of lighter ones. Find a way to appreciate other people's style, vibe, and experience without comparing yourself to them.

Your epic life story resides in your ability to focus on being you and letting everyone else be them.

CONSCIOUSNESS IS COMPLEX

Understanding the complexity of the universe and the entirety of Source is out of the range of our human comprehension, and being okay with that is an agreement we have with Source.

Throughout life, your human mind and body will want to control, understand, logically assess, place blame, and draw conclusions about all the people, places, and things in your experience. Letting those tendencies run wild is what makes life more difficult than it needs to be.

There's a balance that needs to be achieved when awakening to your purpose and your authentic self, a marriage between understanding and relentless Faith. You have to trust that Source's ability to orchestrate opportunities for your highest good is the driving force of life. This combination of understanding where understanding is available—and allowing Faith to support the rest—allows you to receive the knowledge and wisdom you're presented with, while deeply releasing control of outcomes and expectations of what you think should happen with the information you have.

Understanding the world is complex—that you aren't meant to control and understand everything—creates the space needed to have reverence for other people's experiences and of their interpretation of those experiences. There is beauty in our differences and how we all see and interpret the world differently. Admitting the world is complex, that multiple truths can and will exist at the same time, allows you the space to back away from the human urge to be "right" and have somebody else be "wrong."

The complexity of Source is the ability to know and experience everything in your personal world while having no clue what it's like in someone else's.

We can know everything and nothing at the same time.

An area where this agreement comes into play a lot is the human mind's keen ability for making assumptions. Whether it be about assuming what will happen next or what someone's motivations are, even those of us with clear psychic ability are asked to learn to step away from assumptions. Source loves to throw a curveball the second you believe you have everything all figured out. Leaning in to the organized chaos of it all saves a lot of strife, heartache, and headaches along the way.

It's also good to know that because everything is so complex, the challenges you come up against with people and their perception of you isn't personal. Every soul here is operating with their own agenda, their own mission, while working as a piece of the very complex puzzle of the entire experience. Source and you, as the co-creator, are creating—so is everyone else.

Release control. Embrace the complexity and reside in the understanding that everything is working out, especially when it doesn't look like it is. The paths we signed up for are not a straight line. They are an interconnected web of consciousness expressing itself in physical form along the way.

Trust that an amazing, adventurous, beautiful plan was set into motion for you. Let it unfold.

LOVE YOURSELF

Learning to cultivate self-love has a lot of layers. How many layers we work through can be affected by where we started in life—the examples of self-love we had around us, how much our caretakers loved themselves and us—impacts our views of self-love and what we believe is possible for ourselves. The environments you spent your earlier years in impact how many layers you need to unravel to get to the space where you can unconditionally love yourself.

There is no need for guilt or shame for where you start. We all came here with lessons to learn and missions to accomplish. Some of us learn to love ourselves early on—and for those like me, it can take decades. Integrate this truth as you integrate learning to love yourself. You are always exactly where you are meant to be. You can learn to love yourself at 17, or you can start at 70. Either way, it happens exactly on time for your experience.

If you're struggling with self-love, I want you to know that no matter what age you are when you start, the struggle shows you are capable of succeeding. It's an advanced task to start buried underneath the beliefs of unworthiness—and rise to heal yourself through the weight of those beliefs.

Transmuting—alchemizing—the density of a lack of self-love is a massive undertaking. Warriors of Light do this work. They are warriors who come into this world buried under the darkness, because they have the ability to rise through it. Integrate your warrior spirit.

Anchoring in self-love is worth the battle.

Integrate is where your awakening became your life, where the truth of who you are is your practice, and your practice anchors who you are. By showing up for your connection to Source, honoring the agreements we all made before we came here, and learning to live in alignment with your highest, most authentic self, you've created a new foundation—one rooted in truth, balance, and internalized self-respect.

You're no longer awakening; you're becoming the embodiment of all that you've remembered.

But this journey doesn't stop here. *Integrate* opened the doorway to *Expand*, where you stop healing and start fully living. This is the space where you step beyond the internal work and into co-creation with life.

Expand is where you stretch into new possibilities, live in service of something greater, and anchor the frequency of your soul into everything you touch.

You're ready.

You've got this. Keep going.

PART IV

Expand

You've done the deep work.
You've awakened, unraveled,
regulated, and remembered.
You've reconnected with the truth
of who you are, focused on the
layers of your being, and reclaimed
your relationship with Source.
You've come home to yourself.
And now? Now, you *Expand*.

Expansion isn't about doing more. It's not fixing or striving or hustling toward some imagined version of success. Expansion is the natural unfolding that happens when you stop contracting around your wounds and instead live from the frequency of wholeness. It's when your healing becomes your lifestyle, when you walk in alignment, and when the inner transformation—that you've worked so hard for—starts shaping your outer world in ways you can feel, see, and touch.

This section of the book is about that unfolding. It's about understanding the energetic laws that hold the universe together—and how to live in harmony with them. Because once you're anchored in truth, you feel the natural rhythm of things. You see how life isn't just happening *to* you but *through* you. You stop fighting the ebb and flow and move with it instead.

When you *Expand*, you're asked to master the art of balance—light and dark, doing and being, giving and receiving, masculine and feminine. It's through this balance that you step fully into your purpose.

Integrity will be your compass as you *Expand*. It's what keeps your energy clean, your soul grounded, and your vision clear. Without integrity, even the most beautiful spiritual truths can lead you into distortion or illusion. Integrity allows you to own your truth, honor your path, and have the courage to *live* in a way that matches your unique alignment.

Then you'll return to the frequency of Source: love.

Love is a force that reorganizes everything in its presence. When you *Expand* through the frequency of love, you unlock the most powerful potential available to you. Love transforms lack into abundance, fear into courage, confusion into clarity. Love is what softens the heart enough to trust, forgive, and try again.

Through love all is possible.

This isn't the end of your journey. This is another space where beginnings look a lot like endings. *Expand* will ask you to embody a new way of living, loving, and showing up in the world. You are not who you were when you started this book. You're more embodied, more aware, more connected to your soul.

This is where it gets really beautiful.

You've got this. Keep going.

CHAPTER 11

THE BALANCE

Life unfolds as a dance between opposites. From the moment we take our first breath, we are born into a world shaped by contrast—light and dark, joy and sorrow, action and rest. These polarities are not by accident; they're the threads of emotional experience weaving the fabric of existence. Without darkness, light would have no meaning. Without challenge, growth would be impossible.

Yet, we often find ourselves resisting this balance. We cling to the light, striving for ease and certainty, while pushing away the shadows that feel too heavy to bear. But what if the very peace we seek lies not in escaping the tension between the opposites but in embracing them?

Life is not a choice between extremes; it's the spectrum in between. The yin and yang, the masculine and feminine, the expansion and contraction—each is a vital part of the whole. And when we learn to hold space for both, something extraordinary happens. We step into an elevated awareness, one that transcends the need for absolutes and welcomes the fullness of life.

This chapter invites you to explore the delicate art of balance, not as a static goal but as a living, breathing process—a dance that evolves as you evolve. It's about discovering the harmony within yourself, the integration of opposing forces that creates a life of authenticity, clarity, and alignment.

The balance of life is not about perfection. It's about flow. It's about finding ease in the constant push and pull of life, honoring the way opposites enhance each other and trusting that even in the moments of imbalance, there's wisdom to be found.

As we begin this journey into life's polarities, I invite you to let go of any preconceived notions of balance as a destination. Instead, embrace it as a practice, one that illuminates the path to a deeper connection with yourself and the world around you.

You are not here to conquer the spectrum of life. You are here to embody it.

THE NATURE OF DUALITY

Life, at its core, is an interplay of opposites. From the vast expanse of the cosmos to the most intimate aspects of our being, duality shapes the way we perceive, experience, and understand the world. It's the flow of existence—the push and pull of forces that define and enhance one another. Without one, the other would lose its meaning.

We cherish the warmth of the sun because we've felt the chill of the night. We savor moments of joy because we've walked through sorrow. Opposites do not merely co-exist; they amplify one another, offering depth and context that one alone could never provide. Think about the most joyful moment of your life. Perhaps it was the birth of a child, a reunion with a loved one, or a long-awaited achievement. Now imagine that moment if you had never known struggle or loss. Would the joy feel as sweet or the moment as profound? It's in the backdrop of life's shadows that our brightest lights shine. Sorrow makes joy sacred. Darkness gives light its brilliance.

The gift of duality is the contrast and understanding we gain through it.

The human experience is a perfect mirror of this duality. We are beings of both the physical and the spiritual. Our bodies ground us in the tangible, while our souls connect us to the infinite. The mind craves logic and order, while the heart whispers of intuition and feelings that defy explanation. We are constantly navigating this inner balance—the pull between what we can see and what we can sense, between what we know and what we feel.

This internal back and forth can feel overwhelming. *How do you honor both the voice of reason and the whisper of your soul? How do you find balance when your instincts pull you in two directions at once?* These questions are not meant to frustrate you; they are invitations to grow. The tension is not a problem to solve but a mystery to explore.

Nature is the ultimate teacher of duality. Day and night, summer and winter, the ebb and flow of the tides—these cycles are the rhythm of life itself. Day gives us energy and activity; night offers rest and reflection. Summer's abundance teaches us to thrive, while winter's stillness invites us to conserve and prepare. Even the ecosystems that sustain us rely on balance: predator and prey, growth and decay, chaos and order. Remove one, and the delicate equilibrium collapses. All are essential; all are sacred.

And yet, we resist this balance. We cling to the light, to comfort, to certainty, hoping to avoid the shadows that feel too heavy or uncertain. We see duality as a battleground, a place where opposites must fight for dominance. But duality is not meant to divide.

Light and dark are not adversaries in the eyes of Source but collaborators in the grand story of life.

The yin and yang of existence are not sides at war but different expressions of the same whole.

This unity in duality extends to your journey as well. You're not meant to choose between mind and heart, logic and intuition, or physical and spiritual. *The real magic happens when you integrate these aspects of yourself.* When logic collaborates with intuition, decisions are both informed and inspired. When the physical body aligns with the spiritual self, you can experience a profound sense of wholeness.

This is the essence of *unity in duality*. It asks you to soften your grip on the need for absolutes. It invites you to see that opposites are not separate entities but reflections of the same truth. Masculine energy, with its action and drive, is not separate from the feminine energy of intuition and flow—they are two currents of the same river. Expansion and contraction are not opposites but rhythms in the same breath.

In embracing duality, we begin to understand that life's opposites are not obstacles to overcome but opportunities to deepen our awareness. The tension between them is not something to resolve but something to explore. We discover the fullness of who we are when we do.

Duality asks you to trust in the interplay of forces, even when it feels uncomfortable. It teaches you that challenges are not merely tests but invitations to grow. It reminds you that the shadow you fear is the very thing that reveals the brilliance of your light. And in every polarity, there is a lesson—an opportunity to find balance, to honor both sides, and to experience life in its richest, most authentic form.

Take a moment to reflect on the times in your life when you've felt most alive. *Were they the easy, predictable times? Or were they the moments when you stood at the edge of uncertainty, facing both fear and Faith?*

Life's greatest breakthroughs often come when we embrace the tension between opposites—the courage to leap despite the fear, the willingness to heal despite the pain, the choice to love despite the risk of loss.

Nature offers a constant reminder that balance is not static. It's a dynamic process that evolves just as we do. The ocean doesn't apologize for its tides; it surrenders to the push and pull of the moon. The seasons don't cling to one form; they effortlessly move from one to another, knowing that each phase has its purpose. You too are asked to surrender—to trust the rhythms of your life, especially when they take you into the unknown.

Duality is the essence of the human experience. It's not something to conquer or resolve; it's something to embody. To live fully, you embrace the light and the dark, the joy and the sorrow, the known and the mysterious. You learn to trust that every experience, no matter how contradictory it may seem, is a vital part of the whole.

So, as you continue your journey, remember this: The tension between opposites is not a flaw in life's design. It *is* the design. It's what makes life rich, complex, and profoundly beautiful. In the push and pull of duality, there is no winner or loser—only the constant unfolding of truth.

When you embrace this, you step into a deeper harmony with yourself and the world around you. You begin to see that the light within you shines brightest when it has faced its shadows. You begin to trust that every push and pull, every moment of imbalance, is guiding you toward a greater wholeness in yourself and a higher good.

THE DANCE OF MASCULINE AND FEMININE ENERGIES

Within each of us, an interplay of unique energies unfolds—the dance between the masculine and feminine. These energies aren't bound by gender but are universal energetic principles that shape how we create, connect, and experience life. Together, they form the rhythm of existence, where action meets intuition, structure meets flow, and doing meets being. To live fully, we must honor both of these energies; they're two halves of a whole, each incomplete without the other—forever entangled.

Masculine energy is the architect of structure and action. It's the force that builds, protects, and drives progress. Logic, strategy, and discipline are hallmarks of this energy. The masculine turns ideas into tangible results, much like an unbreakable mountain standing firm amid the storms. Rooted in the physical, it thrives in the clarity of goals and the power of determination.

Feminine energy is the essence of flow and creation. It thrives in intuition, empathy, and an embrace of the unknown. This energy moves like a river through a canyon or a fire through the forest—adaptable yet unyielding. The feminine listens to the quiet whispers of the soul, sensing truths that logic cannot grasp. It's the oracle's vision, the energy of inspiration, and the spark from which all life emerges.

But in our world, this delicate balance has not been maintained. We live in an era shaped by patriarchal values that celebrate the masculine while silencing and undervaluing the feminine. Productivity is prized over presence, logic over intuition, and action over rest. "Doing" is rewarded, while "being" is dismissed as lazy or unproductive. This imbalance has suppressed the feminine within individuals and created a collective disconnection from the harmony these energies bring when they work together.

The consequences of this imbalance are everywhere. Exhaustion, burnout, and a sense of inner fragmentation arise when we lean too heavily on masculine energy. Life becomes a checklist, leaving no space for softness or spontaneity. On the other hand, if we lean too deeply into feminine energy without structure, we may feel ungrounded, lost in dreams without the action to manifest them.

Reaching a state of harmony starts with recognizing that the masculine and feminine work best when they collaborate rather than compete—physically and energetically. We don't choose one over the other; we allow them to co-exist through dynamic balance. The dance between these energies is an integration—a conscious effort to honor the gifts of both energies within ourselves.

Living in a world where productivity is idolized makes slowing down feel like a rebellion.

Yet it's in the pause, in the art of being, that we reconnect with the feminine. Balancing the masculine's drive to "do" with the feminine's wisdom of "being" begins with creating intentional space.

> Setting aside 15 minutes a day for reflection, creativity, or stillness can reconnect you with your inner flow. This might look like journaling to process your emotions, meditating to quiet the mind, or taking a walk in nature to let inspiration flow freely. These moments release the need for constant action and allow us to access clarity through connection.

Without the feminine, doing leads to burnout. Without the masculine, being lacks the structure needed to bring ideas to life. True balance comes when we honor both energies—taking inspired action when called to do so and embracing rest as an essential part of the cycle.

Intuition is the voice of the feminine, a deep inner knowing that defies logic and reasoning. Yet, many of us have been conditioned to dismiss it, leaning heavily on the masculine's analytical side. Think of how often you've silenced a gut feeling because it didn't "make sense," only to realize later that your intuition had been right all along.

Balancing logic and intuition begins with trust.

When faced with decisions, pause and ask, "What feels right?" Trust the whispers of your soul, even when they seem irrational. Then use logic to map out the practical steps needed to support your intuitive guidance.

For instance, if intuition nudges you toward a new opportunity but your logical mind raises doubts, allow the two to collaborate. Intuition shows you the path; logic ensures your footing along the way. This integration creates a powerful partnership, where inspired visions are grounded in reality.

The balance of masculine and feminine energies within you extends outward, shaping all your relationships.

When one energy dominates, relationships reflect the imbalance. An overemphasis on masculine energy can lead to rigidity, emotional detachment, and an inability to connect deeply. Conversely, an excess of feminine energy may create passivity, blurred boundaries, or a lack of direction.

Balanced energies, however, bring harmony and depth to our connections. This isn't about adhering to traditional gender roles but about embracing the dance of these energies in ourselves and others.

For example, a relationship thrives when one partner's protective and decisive masculine energy complements the other's empathetic and intuitive feminine energy—and vice versa.

This balance also allows us to communicate with greater clarity and compassion. When we embrace the masculine's strength and the feminine's softness, we create spaces where both feel seen, heard, and supported. These energies exist in all of us, regardless of how our physical bodies present. Learning to balance your internal equilibrium of these energies will allow you to navigate the external world with more ease—operating from your authentic power—and inviting in relationships that complement your balance of these energies.

Harmonizing these energies within yourself transforms the way you show up in the world.

You'll no longer feel the need to overcompensate by hiding parts of who you are. Instead, you can draw on the masculine's courage to speak your truth and the feminine's authenticity to do so with Faith and Grace.

Creativity flourishes in this balance. The feminine energy inspires visions and ideas, while the masculine provides the discipline to bring them into form. Whether you're pursuing art, leadership, or personal goals, this integration empowers you to express yourself in ways that are both bold and meaningful.

Practical Steps

- **Create rituals for balance:** Dedicate time to practices that nurture both energies. For example, balance goal-setting and organizing (masculine) with activities like free writing or dancing (feminine).
- **Practice mindful moments:** Pause throughout the day to tune in. Ask, "What do I need right now?" Whether it's inspired action or rest, honor what arises.

- **Embrace polarity in movement:** Physical practices like yoga, tai chi, or Pilates embody the balance of opposites–masculine strength and feminine fluidity.
- **Set boundaries with compassion:** Let the masculine energy empower you to say no, while the feminine ensures you do so with empathy and understanding.
- **Trust in the cycles:** Just as nature flows through growth and rest, honor your own rhythms. Trust that moments of pause are as valuable as moments of action.

When you find harmony between these energies, you step into the fullness of who you are. You are the creator and the caretaker, the thinker and the dreamer, the builder and the visionary. This balance doesn't ask you to change who you are; it invites you to embrace all that you are.

Where might you invite more balance between doing and being in your life? Take a moment to reflect—and trust in the rhythm of these energies.

THE INNER AND OUTER WORLDS

Life unfolds across two interconnected realms—the inner world, where our thoughts, emotions, and beliefs reside, and the outer world, which encompasses our relationships, work, and the demands of daily life. These realms exist in constant dialogue, each influencing the other. When they are in harmony, we experience flow, fulfillment, and a sense of purpose. But when the balance tips—favoring one realm at the expense of the other—we find ourselves overwhelmed, unfulfilled, or feeling disconnected.

To thrive, we honor both worlds, recognizing their interplay as vital instead of an imposition. Balancing the inner and outer energies requires awareness, intention, and the courage to prioritize what truly aligns with your energy.

Our inner world is the foundation of everything we create and experience.

It's where mindset, emotions, intuition, and self-care converge to shape the lens through which we see the external world. Without tending to this inner realm, your outer actions become reactive and misaligned.

Neglecting the inner world often leads to chaos disguised as busyness. Imagine a tree that grows tall but has shallow roots—it may look strong, but when the storms of life roll in, it can't stand firm. Similarly, if we constantly prioritize the outer world—our obligations, responsibilities, and appearances—over inner nourishment, we risk burnout, emotional dysregulation, and a loss of connection to ourselves.

Nurturing the inner world starts with self-awareness. This means paying attention to the undercurrents of your thoughts and emotions and creating space for practices that sustain you. Meditation, journaling, breath work, and rest are not luxuries; they are necessities. They ground you in your truth and allow you to approach the outer world with clarity and intention.

The outer world is where we express who we are.

It's the realm of action, relationships, and the contributions we make. Here, the energy we cultivate internally flows outward to shape our work, commitments, and connections with others.

When we focus excessively on the outer world, we often fall into the trap of people-pleasing, overworking, and chasing external validation. The demands of work, relationships, and societal expectations can feel relentless, pulling us farther away from ourselves. We become performers in a play we didn't audition for, exhausted by the effort to meet everyone else's needs while ignoring our own.

But the outer world isn't an enemy. It's a vital part of our existence and offers opportunities for growth, joy, and meaningful connection.

The key is to approach it with intention—aligning your actions and choices with your inner values. When the outer world reflects the harmony of your inner world, it becomes a space of empowerment instead of being a drain on your energy.

Imbalance arises when we over-invest in one realm while neglecting the other.

Too much focus on the outer world leads to exhaustion, stress, and a loss of self, while excessive attention to the inner world can result in stagnation, withdrawal, and isolation.

Burnout is a common symptom of outer-world dominance. It manifests as physical fatigue, emotional numbness, and a creeping sense of dissatisfaction, no matter how much we achieve. On the other hand, an overemphasis on the inner world can leave us disconnected from reality, unable to translate insights into action and contribute in a meaningful way to the world around us.

The first step to addressing imbalance is recognizing where it exists. *Are you constantly in "go mode," neglecting time for self-reflection and rest? Or are you so inwardly focused that you struggle to take action or engage with others?* Awareness is the bridge that reconnects these realms, allowing you to recalibrate.

Tools for Balancing the Inner and Outer Worlds

Achieving balance between the inner and outer worlds requires practices that foster harmony. Here are some tools to guide the process:

- **Mindfulness: The Anchor Between Worlds** Mindfulness bridges the gap between inner awareness and outer engagement. It invites you to be fully present—whether you're meditating in solitude or engaging in a conversation. By cultivating mindfulness, you learn to respond to life intentionally rather than reactively, bringing the clarity of your inner world into your external actions. Start small: Take five minutes each morning to tune in to your breath, noticing any thoughts or emotions that arise without judgment. Throughout the day, practice mindfulness by bringing your full attention to everyday tasks—washing dishes, listening to a loved one, or even walking outside.

- **Set Boundaries That Protect Inner Space:** Boundaries are the framework supporting balance. Without them, the outer world encroaches on our inner world, leaving little room for self-care or reflection. Setting boundaries isn't about shutting people out; it's about creating space for what truly matters. Begin by identifying areas where your time and energy feel drained. Is it saying yes too often or taking on responsibilities that aren't yours? Practice saying no with compassion, recognizing that honoring your limits is an act of self-respect that ultimately benefits everyone around you.

- **Prioritize Alignment Over Achievement:** Rather than chasing external achievements for their own sake, focus on actions that align with your values and inner truth. When your outer efforts stem from a place of authenticity, they feel purposeful rather than exhausting. Take time to reflect on what truly matters to you. What brings you joy, fulfillment, and a sense of contribution?

Let these answers guide your decisions, whether in your career, relationships, or daily routines.

- **Create a Daily Ritual for Connection:** Balance doesn't happen by accident; it's cultivated through consistent practice. Dedicate time each day to connect with your inner world before engaging with the outer one. This could be a morning meditation, writing down intentions for the day, or simply sitting quietly with your thoughts before diving into your phone or to-do list. Similarly, create moments throughout the day to pause and recalibrate. These "regroups" allow you to check in with yourself, ensuring you're moving through the world with intention rather than overwhelm.

When you balance your inner and outer worlds, you tap into a state of flow where your internal clarity informs your external actions, and your external experiences enrich your inner growth. You move through life with a sense of alignment, no longer pulled in opposing directions but supported by the harmony of these two realms.

This balance is a dynamic process, not a destination—a balancing act that requires consistent adjustment as life shifts and evolves. There will be times when one realm demands more attention than the other, and that's okay. What matters is the intention to return to center, to recalibrate when needed, and to honor both the inner and outer forces that shape our lives.

You have the tools to navigate this balance. Trust yourself, listen to the whispers of your soul, and take inspired action in the world.

NAVIGATING THE EBB AND FLOW

Balance is often imagined as a perfect, unchanging state—a place we can reach and stay indefinitely. But life doesn't work that way. Balance is not a fixed destination; it's a dynamic, living process. It requires us to adapt to the ebb and flow of life's demands, just as a snowboarder constantly adjusts or a yogi shifts with the slightest change in position. True balance lies in your ability to recalibrate, not in achieving stillness.

Imagine standing on a balance beam. Each step forward requires micro adjustments to your posture, arms, and footing. You may sway to one side, but a quick shift keeps you upright. Balance in life works much the same way. It's not about staying perfectly centered at all times but about recognizing when you're leaning too far in one direction and taking steps to restore the balance.

Chasing a permanent sense of balance can lead to frustration. Life is ever-changing, filled with unexpected twists and turns, opportunities, and challenges. Holding yourself to an ideal of constant equilibrium is like trying to freeze a river in motion—it denies the natural flow of existence.

Instead of striving for perfection, embrace the process of finding continual alignment.

Balance begins with self-awareness. Just as a snowboarder feels the pull of gravity, signaling a need to adjust, we too receive signals when our inner or outer worlds are out of sync. These signals might appear as physical exhaustion, irritability, a lack of motivation, or a nagging sense of unease.

The key is learning to pause and listen. *Are you pushing too hard in your external world—overcommitting, overworking, or overextending? Or are you retreating too deeply into your inner world, avoiding necessary action or connection?* Self-awareness allows you to spot the imbalance before it grows into burnout, disconnection, or dissatisfaction.

Take time each day to check in with yourself. *How does your body feel? What emotions are surfacing? Are you energized or drained by your current activities?* These moments of reflection ensure you're still on the path you intended to walk.

Balance requires flexibility—the willingness to adjust as life changes.

Just like changing or holding a position in yoga, when one side feels heavier, your balance shifts. To restore equilibrium, you shift and move until you find balance once more.

In life, this can mean shifting your priorities. During particularly demanding periods, like a work deadline or caring for a loved one, your outer world may require more attention. During quieter times, you may focus on nourishing your inner world. Neither state is "right" or "wrong." Balance is about honoring what's needed in the present moment while remaining aware of the bigger picture.

Flexibility also means letting go of guilt. When the scales tip, it's easy to feel like you're failing—to keep up, to nurture yourself, or to meet expectations. But imbalance is not failure; it's simply an invitation to recalibrate. By releasing judgment, you create space to course-correct with compassion instead of criticism.

Tools for Navigating the Ebb and Flow

Staying balanced amid life's shifts requires creating a toolkit of practices that keep you anchored in your center. These tools don't guarantee perfection, but they serve as guiding principles in the ebb and flow of life.

- **Anchor yourself in your values**: Your values act as a safety harness when you're out on a limb, keeping you steady as you move forward. When life pulls you in different directions, returning to your core values can help you decide where to focus your energy. Ask yourself: Does this align with what truly matters to me?
- **Embrace rest as a reset button:** Rest is not a retreat; it's a recalibration. Just as a snow globe settles when left alone, taking moments of rest allows you to find your center again. Whether it's a short walk, deep breaths, or a day off, rest renews your ability to engage with both inner and outer worlds.

- **Accept life's imperfections:** Balance isn't about getting everything "right." Sometimes, the best course of action is simply to acknowledge the messiness of life and take the next small step forward. Trust that balance is a process ever unfolding.
- **Prioritize the present moment:** The only place balance truly exists is in the now. By grounding yourself in the present, you can respond to life as it unfolds rather than reacting to fears about the past or future.

The ever-changing nature of balance is what makes it beautiful. It's a reflection of life itself—ever-changing, unpredictable, and filled with opportunities for growth. Each wobble, misstep, and adjustment teaches you something new about yourself and your capacity to navigate the journey here.

As you move through life, it's important to remember balance isn't about staying perfectly still but about staying engaged in the process. Trust in your ability to adjust, listen to the signals of your body and soul and meet each moment with curiosity and compassion.

BALANCE IS A PORTAL OF AWARENESS

Balance isn't about maintaining order in a chaotic world—it's a sanctuary, a refuge we build within ourselves. It's the stillness we crave when life feels overwhelming, the grounding force that keeps us steady when everything seems to pull us in a million different directions. Balance isn't a perfectly orchestrated life—balance aligns us with the energy of Grace as we navigate the imperfections of life.

In the moments when we feel stretched too thin, when the demands of life overshadow our own needs, balance whispers to us: "Come back to center. Remember who you are." This practice of coming back to ourselves—again and again—is where elevated awareness begins. When we choose balance, we step into harmony with the natural rhythms of our life, creating space for clarity, connection, and purpose to emerge.

Have you ever felt so scattered that even small decisions feel monumental? Or so overwhelmed that the noise in your head drowns out your own voice? In these moments, balance is the gift you didn't know you needed.

When your mind is balanced, the storm clouds part, revealing a clear sky. Suddenly, the noise quiets, and you can hear your inner voice—the one that knows the way. Decisions become less about what others expect of you and more about what feels true to you. It's like coming home to yourself, trusting that the answers have been within you all along.

This clarity brings freedom. Instead of reacting to life's chaos, you respond with purpose. Challenges no longer feel insurmountable; they become opportunities to grow and evolve. In balance, even the most difficult moments transform into stepping stones, guiding you toward a deeper understanding of yourself and your path.

Have you ever experienced a moment that felt like magic—when everything aligned so perfectly that it took your breath away? Perhaps you saw a sign at just the right time or felt an unexplainable sense of peace despite the chaos around you. These moments aren't coincidences. They're glimpses of your highest, most authentic self speaking to you, reminding you of your connection to something greater.

Balance is the key to accessing this connection. When you're grounded, the noise of the outside world fades, and you can hear the whispers of your soul. These whispers might come as a gut feeling, a spark of inspiration, or a quiet nudge that guides you toward what truly matters.

In this state, you don't just feel connected to your higher self—you become it. Your actions align with your deepest values, your choices reflect your truest desires, and your life begins to flow with a sense of ease and purpose.

Balance isn't just about feeling better; it's about becoming more of who you truly are.

Think of the last time your emotions felt overwhelming. Maybe it was the weight of sadness, the sting of anger, or the ache of loneliness. In those moments, it can feel like the emotions are going to consume you. But balance offers a different way—a way to hold space for your feelings without being defined by them.

When you're balanced, your emotions become teachers rather than triggers. Sadness shows you where healing is needed. Anger reveals where boundaries must be set. Even fear, as uncomfortable as it is, can guide you toward your deepest truths, leading you to Faith. Balance doesn't erase these emotions; it helps you navigate them with compassion and curiosity.

Through Grace, balance extends to your relationships. When you're balanced, you're able to show up fully for the people you love without losing yourself in the process. You listen with your heart, speak with intention, and create connections that feel authentic and nourishing.

Balance allows you to love others without forgetting to love yourself.

You may not realize it, but your inner balance has the power to change the world. Think about the last time you encountered someone who radiated calm in the midst of chaos. Their presence likely brought you a sense of peace, even if they said nothing at all. This is the energetic effect of balance—when your harmony, your energy, creates harmony in others.

When you choose balance, you're not just doing it for yourself. You're doing it for your family, your friends, and your community. Your balance inspires others to seek their own, creating a wave of transformation that extends far beyond what you can see. Imagine the possibilities if more people embraced this way of being: families that support one another with love and understanding, communities that prioritize collaboration over conflict, and a world that values peace over division.

Your decision to live in balance matters. It's not a small thing; it's a monumental act of service.

Practices to Embrace Balance

Finding balance doesn't mean life will stop being messy–it means you'll have the tools to meet the mess with Grace. Here are a few practices to help you cultivate balance in your daily life:

- **Pause to breathe:** When life feels overwhelming, pause and take a few deep breaths. This simple act grounds you in the present moment and helps you reconnect with your center.
- **Create space for yourself:** Whether it's five minutes of silence in the morning or an hour-long walk in nature, carve out time to tune in to your needs. Balance thrives in the spaces you create for yourself.
- **Honor your energy**: Pay attention to how you spend your energy. *Are you saying yes to things that drain you? Are you neglecting the things that fill you up?* Realigning your energy is a powerful way to restore balance.
- **Practice gratitude**: Gratitude shifts your focus from what's missing to what's present. It helps you find balance between striving for more and appreciating what you already have.

Choosing balance is an act of self-love. It's a way of saying to yourself, "You matter. Your well-being matters." It's a reminder that you don't have to do everything or be everything for everyone. You are enough, just as you are.

When you prioritize balance in your life, you give yourself permission to rest, to heal, to grow. You become a source of light, not just for yourself but for everyone around you. Your balance inspires others to find their own, creating a wave of harmony that reaches farther than you'll ever know.

Life will never stop being unpredictable.

There will always be challenges, uncertainties, and moments that test your resolve. But when you walk the path of balance, you walk it with the knowledge that you are never alone.

The universe supports you. Your higher self guides you. And every step you take toward balance brings you closer to the truth of who you are. We can create a world where harmony isn't just an ideal—it's a way of life.

You are already enough. You are already whole. All you need to do is come back to center.

Life is a beautiful contradiction. It asks us to be strong, yet reminds us to surrender. It demands action but whispers for stillness. To grow, we must rest. To gain control, we must let go. These contrasts are not obstacles to overcome—they're invitations to expand our understanding of what it means to live authentically and fully.

At first, the contradictions of life can feel maddening. *How do you hold both effort and ease? How do you trust the flow of life while still steering your ship?* But the truth is, we didn't agree to choose one over the other—Source asks us to embrace both. The magic lies not in solving the contradiction but in surrendering to its wisdom.

Imagine trying to grasp water in your hands. The tighter you clench your fists, the more it slips away. But when you soften your grip and cup your hands gently, the water remains. Life's the same. The more we try to control, the more elusive peace becomes. Yet when we hold space for the contradictions, we find a deeper truth waiting for us in the stillness.

One of life's greatest lessons is that in order to gain control, we must first let go.

This seems counterintuitive, especially in a world that praises hustle and mastery. But think about the moments when you've tried to force something—a relationship, a career move, or even a personal goal. The harder you pushed, the farther away it seemed to drift. Then, at the moment you released your grip and surrendered, things began to fall into place effortlessly.

Letting go isn't about giving up; it's about giving over. It's about trusting that there is a rhythm to life that knows the way, even when we can't see the path. When we release our need to control every outcome, we open ourselves to possibilities we couldn't have imagined. Surrender is a doorway, not a defeat.

To grow, we must rest.

In a culture that glorifies productivity, rest is often seen as laziness, an indulgence we can't afford. But nature tells a different story. Think of the winter when the trees appear barren and lifeless. Beneath the surface the roots grow deeper, preparing for the explosion of life in spring. Without rest, there is no growth.

When we honor the need for rest—whether it's physical, emotional, or spiritual—we honor our natural cycles. Rest doesn't take us away from your goals; it realigns you with them. It's in the moments of stillness that clarity emerges, ideas blossom, and energy renews. Growth isn't about constant movement—but about movement with intentional pauses that allow you to recalibrate and rise stronger.

The most profound transformations happen when you learn to hold space for life's tensions without needing to resolve them. Consider the energy of love: It asks you to be vulnerable yet strong. To give, yet also receive. When you try to resolve this tension—by either closing yourself off or giving too much of yourself—you lose the essence of love itself. But when you hold space for both, love becomes expansive . . . infinite.

Holding space for contradiction doesn't mean you need all the answers. It means allowing yourself to sit with the questions and trust the unfolding of life. It's about recognizing that the light needs the shadow, that joy is sweeter because you've known sorrow, and that every ending carries the seed of a new beginning.

When we embrace life's paradoxes, we stop fighting against the current. We learn to flow with it, trusting that even in the contradictions, there is harmony. In this space, you find peace—not in resolution of "life's problems" but in acceptance of how they naturally work themselves out.

Balance is not a destination; it's a journey, of an ever-changing ebb and flow of opposites.

We don't erase life's polarities or achieve a perfect state of equilibrium either. Instead, we learn to move gracefully between the extremes, finding harmony in the interplay of light and dark, effort and ease, control and surrender.

The wisdom you've explored in this chapter reminds you that life's polarities aren't battles to be won or opposites to conquer. They're two sides of the same coin, forces that, when embraced, create a fuller, richer experience of life.

Balance is the higher path—a sacred space where opposites co-exist, enriching one another.

Walking the higher path requires you to release the illusion of perfection. You let go of getting everything right and show up authentically, even when life feels messy. Balance is about knowing that some days will feel harmonious, while others will feel chaotic—and that's okay.

In this acceptance, you'll find freedom. You'll stop striving for a life that looks balanced and start living a life that feels balanced. You'll let go of the appearance of calm while embodying the inner knowing that you are grounded, no matter what comes your way.

Balance is achieved through the small, intentional choices you make each day—pausing to breathe when you feel stress, creating space for what nourishes you, and honoring the rhythm of your energy.

It's in moments of awareness where balance comes alive. When we practice balance, we align with the truth of who we are. We become more attuned to our higher selves, more present in our relationships, and more connected to the world around us. The harmony we cultivate within radiates outward, creating an energy that touches everyone we encounter.

As you walk the higher path of balance, trust that you are exactly where you need to be. Every step you take toward harmony, no matter how small, is a step toward a life of greater peace, purpose, and connection. Even when the path feels uncertain, even when you feel you've fallen and are struggling to get back up.

Life will always be filled with opposites—light and dark, joy and sorrow, effort and ease. But when you embrace these polarities, you discover the profound truth that they aren't separate—they are one. And in their union, you find the energy of balance.

You are already enough. You are already whole.

You've got this, keep going.

CHAPTER 12

INTEGRITY

Integrity is the bridge between who we are and who we are meant to be. It's the quiet, unwavering force that keeps us grounded in our highest truths, even when the world tempts us to stray. At its core, integrity is the alignment of our actions, words, and choices with the authenticity of our soul. It's not just a moral compass—it's the voice of our higher selves, encouraging us to honor the life we've been called to live.

Living in integrity is a return to wholeness. You're asked to strip away the masks you've been taught to wear and embrace the raw, unpolished truth of who you are. When you live in your integrity, you create a vibrational resonance connecting you to something far greater than yourself—a higher aligned reality: Source.

Integrity is how you keep your soul's promises alive, not just in thought but in action. When we live out of alignment with our integrity, the effects are immediate, even if we don't always recognize them. We feel fragmented, because we are. Every decision out of alignment throws pieces of us into the shadow, scattered and disconnected. We can experience a gnawing sense of unease, that whispers, "Something isn't right."

This disconnection and scattering of our self erodes our self-respect and dims our inner light. Without integrity, trust becomes impossible—trust in ourselves, trust in others, and even trust in the path ahead. The irony is that by avoiding the discomfort of standing in our truth, we create a deeper suffering for ourselves: the pain of living a life that isn't fully ours.

Yet when we live in alignment with our integrity, the opposite becomes true. We feel whole. Our energy flows freely because we're no longer at war with ourselves. Decisions, no matter how difficult, carry clarity because they are rooted in what feels right, not what feels easy.

Use integrity like a guide, reminding you that you are capable of living in alignment with the highest version of yourself.

INTEGRITY MATTERS

Integrity isn't a luxury—it's a necessity. It's the foundation that everything meaningful is built on. Self-respect begins with honoring the commitments we make to ourselves. Trust, whether in relationships or in our connection to Source, begins with knowing we are standing in our truth. Your purpose will become clearer when you live in alignment with the values that resonate within you.

The world we live in challenges this alignment. It's filled with external expectations, cultural norms, and the voices of others who tell us who we should be and how we should live. But integrity asks you to step away from these external pressures and turn inward. Integrity doesn't mean we live an idolized life—it's about honesty, with ourselves and everyone around us. It means living in a way that reflects your values, even when it's inconvenient or unpopular.

Living in integrity isn't always easy. It demands courage—the courage to disappoint others, to face your fears, and to let go of what does not align with your truth. But it also offers something immeasurable in return: peace. When you live in integrity, you are able to look in the mirror and see someone you respect. You can rest at night knowing you've honored and aligned with your highest, most authentic self.

In this chapter, we'll explore the journey of living in integrity in a world that will ask you to compromise. We'll look at the ways external expectations and internal fears can pull you away from your truth—and how you can navigate these challenges with the energy of Grace and Faith.

You'll learn how integrity connects you to your sacred contracts, the agreements, the bargains, you made with Source before stepping into this life. We'll discuss how to realign when you stray, how to honor your truth even when it feels uncomfortable, and how integrity creates an energetic effect that transforms not only your life but also the lives of those around you.

Living with integrity doesn't create a perfect life; it creates an authentic one.

You'll learn to trust yourself again, to honor your agreements with Source and yourself, and to walk through life with the unshakable knowing that you're aligned with your highest truth.

Let this chapter be your guide—a reminder that integrity is not something to strive for but something to return to. It's your natural state, your soul's way of being. And in living in integrity, you'll find not only yourself but also the life you were always meant to live.

Integrity is often reduced to a simple definition: honesty. But spiritually, it is far deeper than that.

Integrity is the quantum thread that aligns your actions, words, and intentions with the deepest truths of your soul.

It's devotion to honoring the energy of who you are and the life you came here to live. It's not just about telling the truth—it's about *being* the truth, embodying it fully even when no one else is watching.

At its core, integrity is the bridge that connects us to Source. Each time we act in alignment with our truth, we honor our connections and affirm our soul's purpose. Conversely, when we stray from integrity—when we choose convenience over authenticity or silence over courage—we weaken that connection. This disconnection doesn't punish us, but it does create distance, making it harder to feel the guidance and support of Source in our daily lives.

Integrity is intentional even through imperfection. It's the practice of realigning with your highest truth, even after you misstep. The moments you choose integrity, especially in the face of fear or resistance, are the moments when you reaffirm your partnership with the divine, where you strengthen your connection.

Living in integrity is not just a moral choice—it's an energetic one. When you align with your truth, you create a harmonious resonance that radiates through life. This resonance attracts clarity, abundance, and peace, because the energy you're emitting is consistent with the energy you desire to receive.

On the other hand, betrayal—whether of yourself or others—creates dissonance. This dissonance isn't always immediately apparent, but it manifests as restlessness, anxiety, and a feeling of being "off." It's the heaviness we carry when our actions don't align with our values, the subtle discomfort of knowing we've strayed from our path.

Integrity acts as a stabilizing force in the midst of life's uncertainties. It's a compass, grounding us when external circumstances threaten to pull us in conflicting directions. When we stand in integrity, we can face challenges with clarity, knowing that we are anchored in what is true for us. Even when the path ahead is unclear, integrity assures us that we are moving in alignment with the highest good.

Living in integrity is simple, but it's not always easy.

The world around you will constantly test your commitment to authenticity. Societal pressures urge you to conform. Fear of judgment tempts you to present a polished version of yourself rather than the raw truth. And convenience often lures us into compromises that feel small but carry significant energetic consequences.

One of the most pervasive challenges is the belief that small misalignments don't matter. We tell ourselves that skipping a promise we made to ourselves—whether it's committing to rest, speaking up, or setting a boundary—is insignificant. But these seemingly minor choices accumulate, creating a gap between who we are and who we strive to be. Over time, they erode your self-respect and create patterns of disconnection.

Consider this: Saying yes when you mean no may seem like a small compromise, but it says to your soul that its truth is less important than the comfort of others. Choosing to stay silent when your intuition nudges you to speak up may feel safer in the moment, but it diminishes your trust in your inner voice. These small betrayals anchor timelines, subtly altering the course of your life until the dissonance and disconnection becomes undeniable.

Living in integrity often requires going against the grain. It asks that you prioritize authenticity over acceptance, and that can be terrifying. The world rewards conformity, and standing in your truth can feel isolating at times. But the cost of compromise is far greater than the discomfort of standing alone. The truth is, every decision either brings you closer to or farther from alignment. There is no neutral ground when it comes to integrity. By recognizing the moments when you are tempted to stray—when fear, convenience, or external pressure seeks to dictate your choices—you gain the power to choose differently.

Living in integrity is not about avoiding missteps; it's about learning to course-correct when you do.

Integrity teaches you to become aware of the dissonance, the disconnection, and shows you steps to take to realign with your truth. In doing so, you not only honor your soul's commitments but also create a life of harmony, trust, and fulfillment.

RECOGNIZING MISALIGNMENT

Misalignment whispers before it screams. It begins as a barely noticeable discomfort—a faint sense that something isn't right, even when everything on the surface appears fine. You might feel it in your body: a tightness in your chest, an uneasy knot in your stomach, or a restlessness no amount of distraction can quiet. These physical sensations are the body's way of signaling that something within you is out of alignment.

Emotionally, misalignment speaks the language of anxiety, guilt, and inner conflict. You may find yourself second-guessing decisions or feeling irritable for reasons you can't quite pinpoint. This sense of being "off" often follows you like a shadow, a subtle reminder that you've veered from your truth. It's not always dramatic—sometimes, it's just a quiet voice in the background, asking, *Is this really the life you want to live?*

One of the clearest signs of misalignment is avoidance. You know something isn't right but don't want to face it, so you instinctively look for ways to distract yourself. Maybe you procrastinate on having an honest conversation, delay making a decision, or bury yourself in work to avoid confronting what your intuition is trying to tell you. Avoidance is often a form of self-protection, a way of shielding ourselves from the discomfort of acknowledging where we've strayed.

Then there's self-sabotage, misalignment's most insidious companion. When we betray our own truths, we subconsciously create obstacles that prevent us from moving forward. This might look like overcommitting to things that don't align with your priorities, staying in relationships that drain you, or numbing your feelings with unhealthy habits. These patterns aren't random—they're the soul's way of crying out for realignment, even if it doesn't feel that way at the time.

Living out of integrity comes at a cost, and the price is often paid in silence.

One of the first things to erode is self-trust. Every time you ignore your intuition, make a choice that contradicts your values, or prioritize external validation over your inner truth, you send yourself a message: *Your voice doesn't matter.* Over time, this creates a disconnect between you and your soul, making it harder to access your inner guidance and navigate life with clarity.

Misalignment doesn't just affect your relationship with yourself—it also moves out into your connections with others as well. Authentic relationships require vulnerability and honesty, but when you're out of alignment, it becomes difficult to show up fully. You might find yourself withdrawing emotionally, overcompensating by people-pleasing, or projecting your frustrations onto loved ones. These dynamics create distance and misunderstandings, leaving you feeling isolated even when you're surrounded by people.

Energetically, living out of alignment creates blocks that disrupt the flow of your life. Imagine a river with debris clogging its path. The water still flows, but it's slower, less vibrant, and unable to reach its full potential. Likewise, when you ignore your truths, your energy becomes stagnant. Opportunities that once felt effortless begin to slip through your fingers. Synchronicities—the moments of divine timing reminding you that you're on the right path—become less frequent. Life starts to feel heavy, as if you're pushing against a current instead of flowing with it.

The costs of misalignment are not punishments; they're wake-up calls. The discomfort you feel is not meant to shame you but to guide you back to your center. It's Source's way of saying, "There's a better way, a truer path—will you listen?"

Recognizing misalignment requires courage and radical honesty. It's not always easy to admit where we've strayed from our truths, especially when those choices were made out of fear, convenience, or a desire to avoid conflict. But the first step toward realignment is awareness.

Take a moment to reflect on these questions:

- **What situations or relationships leave you feeling drained or uneasy?**
  Do you feel a knot of tension in your stomach when you agree to plans you don't want to follow through on? Do you dread certain interactions because they require you to suppress your authentic self?

- **Where in your life do you feel like you're "playing small"?**
  Are there areas where you're holding back your truth, either because you fear judgment or because it feels easier to blend in?

- **What commitments have you made that no longer feel aligned?**
  Are you staying in a job, relationship, or routine out of obligation rather than desire?

- **When have you avoided taking action out of fear?**
  Think about the moments when your intuition nudged you to act, but you chose to ignore it.

These questions are not meant to create guilt but to illuminate the areas where you have the opportunity to grow.

Misalignment is not a permanent state—it's an invitation to course-correct, to remember who you are and what you stand for.

Consider this: Imagine saying yes to a request you didn't have the capacity to fulfill. Maybe it was a small favor, like agreeing to help a friend when you were already stretched thin. On the surface, it seems insignificant. But beneath that yes lies a deeper message: Your needs are less important than others' expectations. Over time, these small compromises accumulate, creating a gap between who you are and who you want to be.

Think about a time when you stayed silent instead of speaking your truth. Maybe it was in a meeting where you had an idea but feared it would be dismissed. Maybe it was with a loved one, when you chose peace over honesty. These moments may feel safer in the short term, but they come at the cost of your self-expression. Every time you silence yourself, you diminish your trust in your voice.

While misalignment can be painful, it is also one of life's greatest teachers.

It shines a light on the areas where you've been living out of habit rather than intention, where fear has overshadowed Faith, and where external expectations have taken precedence over your inner knowing. Each moment of misalignment carries a lesson, if you're willing to listen. It's an opportunity to pause, reflect, and ask yourself: What is this discomfort trying to show me? When you approach misalignment with curiosity instead of judgment, you unlock its potential to guide and transform you.

Realigning with integrity is not about erasing the past or pretending you've never strayed. It's about acknowledging where you are now, understanding the choices that brought you here, and taking intentional steps toward a more authentic path.

And here's the beautiful truth: Every step you take toward realignment strengthens your connection to your higher self and Source. The courage to face your misalignment with honesty is the first act of integrity. It's a declaration to the universe that you are ready to live in alignment with your truth, no matter how challenging it may feel.

THE POWER OF LIVING IN INTEGRITY

Living in integrity is about liberation—the freedom to be exactly who you are without apology or compromise. When your actions align with your core values, life becomes simpler and more fluid. Choices that once felt heavy or confusing are suddenly clear because you're no longer in conflict with yourself.

Living in this alignment isn't always easy. The world will demand that you conform, contort, or abandon pieces of yourself to fit in. Living in integrity requires courage—the kind that pushes you to step out of the expectations of others and into the authenticity of your own being. It means choosing truth over comfort, even when that truth shakes the foundations of the life you've built.

I had a client who realized he had been lying to himself for years. His corporate job, while financially rewarding, had drained him to the point of near exhaustion. He felt trapped by this level of success, terrified of losing what he'd worked so hard to achieve. But deep down, he knew he was living a life that wasn't his. He made the terrifying yet liberating choice to leave his job and started his own business—a venture that felt aligned with his heart. The decision wasn't easy, but he discovered a sense of purpose and fulfillment that financial success alone could never provide. *The universe rose to meet him in this alignment, proving abundance can be found by moving in your soul's integrity.*

Living in integrity isn't a single large act most of the time; it's a practice, a series of small, consistent choices that honor who you are. With each decision, you strengthen the bridge between your current self and the person you're meant to become. The clarity that follows isn't intellectual; it's spiritual and it's energetic. It's the peace you find when you know you're showing up to life as your truest self.

Integrity has a magnetic quality.

When you live in alignment, you create a vibrational frequency that attracts what you truly desire—opportunities, relationships, and experiences resonating with your highest good. The universe rewards your authenticity by bringing you closer to your desires—integrity is a tuning fork. When it vibrates clearly, it calls forth a harmonious response from the world around you. This is why alignment is so crucial to manifestation. You can't call in the life you desire if your inner world is in chaos and disarray.

I witnessed this shift through a soul I was supporting. For years, she felt stuck in a cycle of toxic relationships. No matter how hard she tried, she kept attracting partners who mirrored her deepest insecurities. Then, she shifted. She began the process of self-reflection and healing, uncovering the ways she had been betraying herself by settling for less. As she worked to rebuild her sense of self-worth, she found the courage to set firm boundaries and align her actions with her newfound values. It was only then, in the space of her own integrity, that she met a partner who treated her with the love and respect she had always longed for. This wasn't a coincidence. It was the natural result of alignment—her external reality reflecting the truth of her inner world.

When your thoughts, words, and actions align with your core truths, you become a clear channel for divine energy. Integrity allows your desires to flow effortlessly toward you. You don't need to chase or force; your authenticity in your integrity does the attracting for you.

Every promise you make—to yourself, to others, and to the universe—is a sacred agreement.

These commitments are not just words; they're spiritual bargains that shape the trajectory of your life. Living in integrity means honoring these contracts, not out of obligation but out of a reverence for the divine orchestration that happens when you keep your promises.

Think of the commitments you've made to yourself. Maybe you promised to prioritize your health after years of neglect, to honor your creative gifts, or to leave a situation that no longer serves your highest good. These promises are not small—they are acts defining your belief in your own worth and potential. When you follow through, you strengthen your relationship with yourself. You learn to trust your own word, and in doing so, you build a foundation of self-respect that cannot be shaken. Breaking these promises, however, creates fractures—not only in your relationship with yourself but also in your energetic field. These fractures manifest as doubt, confusion, and a sense of being out of alignment with life. The good news is that every moment offers new opportunities to repair these fractures by recommitting to your truth.

These agreements extend beyond yourself to the relationships you hold dear. Whether it's a marriage, a friendship, or a professional partnership, each bond carries the weight of standing in integrity. This doesn't mean staying in relationships that no longer serve you—it means approaching every interaction with honesty and respect. Even when endings are necessary, they can be handled with the energy of Grace, honoring the relationship for what it taught you.

Leaving a relationship that no longer aligns with your truth can be one of the hardest things to do. But you honor all parties involved when you stand in your integrity with what is in alignment and what isn't. While difficult, you create the freedom for everyone involved to meet an aligned path.

Living in integrity requires Faith.

It's a practice of trust when you honor your commitments, aligning yourself with the divine timing of life. And when you fall out of alignment—as we all do—it's about having the courage to course-correct, knowing that Grace is always available when you return to your truths. Integrity isn't just about morality or principles; it's about liberation and authenticity. It's the foundation for a life that feels aligned, authentic, and deeply fulfilling. Living in integrity allows you to walk through the world with clarity and confidence, knowing you are not just existing but thriving in harmony with your purpose.

The path of integrity may not always be easy, but it is always worth it. Each step you take in alignment brings you closer to the life you were meant to live. And as you walk this path, you become a beacon of light, not just for yourself but for everyone around you—a living testament to the power of authenticity and the divine magic of alignment.

Living in integrity doesn't mean you have a "perfect" solution for every problem. And it's definitely not about adhering to a rigid code of conduct that leaves no room for error or human complexity.

Integrity is about honest effort, self-awareness, and showing up authentically, even when life throws you into the gray areas.

Life can be messy, unpredictable, and full of moral dilemmas that rarely offer clear-cut solutions. In these moments, integrity becomes less about always being "right" and more about staying connected to your highest truth. It's about asking yourself, "What is the most aligned action I can take right now, given my circumstances?"

I helped navigate this energy when a woman I guided faced this gray space when her aging parents needed her care, but she was also juggling raising two young children and having a demanding career. She felt torn between her responsibilities and her own well-being. In the past, she would've pushed herself to exhaustion, believing that sacrificing her needs was the only "right" thing to do. But this time, she approached the situation differently. She chose to be honest—with herself and her family. She acknowledged her limitations and sought help, finding a solution that honored her responsibilities while allowing her to maintain her energy.

Her choice wasn't perfect, and there were moments of guilt and doubt. But she learned that living in integrity sometimes means embracing imperfection and trusting that doing your best is enough. It's about finding alignment in the chaos, knowing that your truth may evolve as you navigate through situations in your life.

Boundaries are an essential, yet often overlooked, part of integrity.

Boundaries aren't separations from others but bridges connecting you to your highest, most authentic self. When you set boundaries, you're saying, "I value myself enough to honor what I need to thrive." Integrity often requires saying no to others so you can say yes to yourself. This isn't selfish—it's self-respect. We can't pour from an empty cup. Without boundaries, you risk depleting yourself to meet the needs of others, leaving nothing for your own well-being.

One of the most profound lessons in boundaries comes when we realize they not only protect us but also teach others how to treat us.

When a member of my community shared how she was struggling with her boss, who routinely piled extra work onto her plate, I encouraged her to set boundaries. For years, she stayed silent, fearing conflict and wanting to appear as a team player. But the constant overwork took a toll on her health and happiness. When she finally decided to have a direct conversation with her boss, she was terrified. But to her surprise, her honesty was met with respect. By standing in her integrity and expressing her limits, she not only reclaimed her time but also cultivated a deeper sense of self-worth. Boundaries, she realized, are an act of alignment—a way of living in truth with what she can and cannot give.

Integrity isn't a fixed state; it's a journey that will include moments of misalignment.

You will make mistakes. You will act out of fear, doubt, or be impulsive at times. This doesn't mean you've failed. It simply means you're human.

The power of integrity lies in your willingness to course-correct when you've veered off track. Meet those moments with compassion and the courage to try again.

One of the most powerful ways to move back into integrity is through acknowledgment. Whether it's an apology to someone you've wronged or a commitment to yourself that you've neglected, owning your actions is the first step toward healing.

I worked with a woman who had distanced herself from a close friend after a rather large argument. Months passed, and the silence between them grew heavier. She missed her friend but was afraid to reach out, fearing rejection or an even deeper rift. After we spoke, and feeling through the alignment, she decided to reach out. She admitted her role in the conflict, expressed her genuine regret, and shared her desire to repair the relationship. Her friend responded with Grace and vulnerability, and they rebuilt their connection stronger than before because she had the courage to stand in her truth and make amends.

Integrity doesn't demand perfection. It asks for authenticity, effort, and the humility to admit when you've fallen short. Each time you course-correct, you strengthen your foundation and show yourself—and others—that integrity is a living, breathing practice of alignment.

Practical Tools for Stepping Back into Integrity

When you've stepped out of alignment, whether with yourself or others, here are some tools to help you return to your center:

- **Reflection:** Take time to pause and reflect on where you went off course. Ask yourself, "What led me here? What truth did I ignore or deny?" Clarity begins with self-awareness.
- **Acknowledge without judgment**: Accept your actions without harsh self-criticism. Integrity thrives in an environment of compassion, not shame.
- **Take responsibility:** If your actions affected others, be willing to own your part. A sincere apology can go a long way in mending trust.

- **Recommit to your values:** Use the experience as a reminder of what truly matters to you. Reconnect with your core truths and let them guide your next steps.
- **Be patient with the process:** Rebuilding trust, whether with yourself or others, takes time. Allow space for healing to unfold naturally.

Each moment offers an opportunity to live in truth, to set boundaries, to course-correct, and to honor the sacred agreements we hold with ourselves and the world around us.

When we navigate the gray areas with honesty and Grace, we discover that integrity isn't about always getting it right—it's about freedom.

The freedom to be human, to learn from your missteps, and to keep choosing alignment, again and again.

Living in alignment with integrity is an ongoing journey—a commitment to show up for yourself and others with truth and authenticity. Integrity doesn't happen in bursts of grandeur or picture-perfect steps. It's found in the quiet moments when no one is watching, in the small, steady choices that, over time, shape the essence of who you are. Each day offers a chance to lean in to alignment, to repair what's been misaligned, and to step closer to the version of yourself you know you were born to be.

There is a certain kind of bravery required to look inward, to ask yourself hard questions, and to face what you find without judgment.

Introspection is a doorway to alignment. Journaling becomes a mirror, reflecting not only your deepest truths but also the places where you've strayed from them. A friend of mine shared that through her daily journaling practice, she realized she'd been living according to others' expectations for years. Writing her truth on paper gave her the clarity and courage to begin reclaiming her life—one aligned decision at a time. You can use this tool too.

Sit quietly with a journal in your lap and pour your thoughts onto the page: Where do I hold back? Where am I living out of fear rather than love? These questions crack open the places in your life where integrity is asking to take root.

A daily meditation practice is like an anchor in a storm. A few minutes of mindful breathing can change the course of your day. When you're present, you act from a place of truth rather than reaction. That pause can be the difference between a decision you regret and one that brings peace to your soul.

Close your eyes, breathe, and return to stillness. Mindfulness practices and meditation bring you back to center, to that unshakable part of you that already knows what's right.

Life can be noisy—full of distractions, opinions, and demands pulling you in every direction. But when you close your eyes, breathe, and return to stillness, you remember. You remember who you are, what matters and where your next step lies.

There's a moment in every journey when you're asked to stand in your truth, even when your voice shakes and your body is trembling.

Speaking your truth doesn't mean being harsh—it's about allowing your authenticity to rise to the surface with compassion and love. It's the gentle but firm no when someone asks for more than you can give. It's the honest conversation with a loved one when something isn't working.

The woman I worked with who reached out to her friend to repair their relationship also wrestled with expressing her needs. She feared losing the friendship, but holding back how she was really feeling left her feeling unseen and drained. When she finally found the courage to speak, her vulnerability deepened their bond. "For the first time," she told me, "I felt like I could be myself and still be loved." That's the power of living in integrity—it liberates not only you but those around you too, creating deeper, more meaningful relationships.

Integrity isn't measured by monumental acts; it's etched in the fabric of your everyday life. It's the seemingly insignificant decisions that reveal your character and solidify your alignment with your highest, most authentic self.

There's the beauty of integrity in the smallest of choices.

It's returning a shopping cart to the rack because you value respect for others' time. It's calling a friend to apologize, even when it feels awkward, because the relationship means more than your pride. These small moments may seem insignificant, but they create a life built on trust, authenticity, and alignment.

I coached someone who, for years before working with me, stayed silent when unethical practices occurred around her at work, believing it wasn't her place to speak up, until she couldn't ignore it anymore and asked for guidance moving forward. She chose to raise her voice—not in anger but with clarity and conviction in her soul's truth. Her actions inspired others to do the same, creating a culture shift in her company. Never doubt that small choices, when made with integrity, carry extraordinary power.

When you live with integrity, something magical happens—you learn to trust yourself.

The small choices you make every day build the foundation of a life you can be proud of. Over time, this trust becomes unshakable.

Weave integrity into the tapestry of your life. Each day you add another stitch, creating an energy that is strong, beautiful, and uniquely yours. Steady, deliberate actions align you with your highest truth. Peace comes when you know you're living in alignment. Each day, integrity invites you to step into freedom. The freedom to live authentically, to honor your truth, and to move through life with a quiet but unshakable confidence.

So, start today. Breathe into the moment, reconnect with what matters most, and take one small, aligned step forward. It doesn't have to be a giant gesture—it just has to be honest.

Because in the end, integrity isn't just something you practice. It's who you are. *And who you are is enough.* You create unseen energetic waves with every choice, every word, every action. Your energy is like a stone tossed into a still pond. It ripples out, spreading far beyond the initial splash, reaching shores you cannot see.

When you choose to live authentically, the people around you feel it. They sense the steadiness in your presence, the truth in your words, and the clarity in your actions. That kind of energy is magnetic. It inspires others to reflect on their own lives and ask, "Am I living in alignment with who I truly am?"

Consider the small, everyday moments when someone else's integrity has shifted something in you. Perhaps it was a friend who admitted a mistake instead of making excuses, teaching you that vulnerability is strength. Or a colleague who stood up for what was right, even when it cost them, reminding you that courage is contagious. These acts of integrity light a spark in others, inviting them to rise to their highest potential.

Now imagine what happens when entire communities commit to integrity—when trust becomes the foundation of relationships, when people lead with their hearts instead of their egos, and when authenticity is celebrated rather than feared.

Integrity creates an energy of unity, breaking down barriers and building bridges. It reminds us that we are all connected, and our choices don't just affect our lives—they move through the collective consciousness.

In a private session, a client of mine shared that after years of hiding her truth in fear of being judged, she made the brave decision to live authentically. She began speaking honestly with her loved ones, owning her mistakes, and showing up fully as herself. She told me, "I thought people would reject me, but instead, they started opening up in ways I'd never seen before. It was like my truth gave them permission to share theirs." Her integrity didn't just transform her—it transformed her relationships and became a source of healing for everyone around her.

This is the larger impact of integrity: It's not just a gift you give yourself—it's a gift you give the world.

Living in integrity isn't always easy. There will be moments when choosing your truth feels like walking into the fire. You may question yourself, wondering if the discomfort is worth it. This is where Faith becomes your guide. Faith whispers, "Even if you can't see the outcome, trust you're on the right path." Faith and integrity are deeply intertwined.

Integrity asks you to honor your truth, even when the road ahead is unclear. Faith reminds you that aligning with your truth is never in vain—that the universe moves in ways you may not yet understand, orchestrating a bigger picture than you can see.

Trusting in divine timing is not always easy, especially when the stakes are high. Perhaps you've had to walk away from a relationship that no longer served you or speak up in a situation where silence would have been safer. These moments test your resolve, but they also strengthen your connection to Source.

I've seen this play out time and again with those who face crossroads in their lives. A woman I guided spent years in a career that drained her, and for her spirit's sake, she found the courage to leave. It wasn't an easy decision—she worried about finances, stability, and how others would perceive her. But she trusted her intuition, and as she aligned with her truth, opportunities began to unfold that she never could have predicted. "It felt like the universe was waiting for me to take that first step," she told me. And it is.

Faith doesn't promise that the path will be smooth, but she does promise that every step taken in alignment with your sou'ls truth will lead you closer to your purpose.

When you align Faith with integrity, you walk through life with a sense of quiet confidence, knowing that you are supported—no matter what the world around you looks like.

Integrity is a practice. There will be days when you falter, when fear or doubt creeps in, and that's okay. Living in integrity doesn't mean you never stray—it means you always find your way back.

Each day offers a fresh opportunity to begin again. Perhaps you start small, with a single act of alignment: speaking your truth in a conversation, honoring a boundary you've set, or choosing kindness over judgment. These small acts are like drops of water, steadily filling a well of trust within you. Over time, this well becomes a source of resilience. You learn to trust yourself more deeply. You begin to see how your daily choices weave together to create a life that feels whole, authentic, and aligned.

A member of mine shared a metaphor that captures this beautifully. She said, "Living in integrity feels like building a house brick by brick. Some days it feels slow, but then you look back and realize you've built something solid—something that can weather any storm." This is the path forward: to treat each day as an opportunity to lay another brick, to choose alignment even when it's hard, and to trust that the life you're building is one of truth and purpose.

As you continue this journey, remember that integrity is about showing up with an open heart, a willingness to learn, and a commitment to grow.

At its core, integrity is a connection to your higher self, to the sacred contracts you carry, and to the divine energy within you.

It's a compass that guides you back to your truth, time and time again. When you live in integrity, you become a vessel for something greater. You inspire others to rise, you contribute to the healing of the collective, and you strengthen your connection to Source. This isn't just about living a good life—it's about living a meaningful one, a life that aligns with the truth of who you are.

So, take a moment today to reconnect with your inner most compass. Close your eyes, breathe deeply, and ask yourself: What is my next aligned step?

Because in the end, integrity is a way of being. It's a promise you make to yourself—and to the world—that you will show up authentically, courageously, and fully. And when you live with that kind of truth, you don't just navigate life—you transform it.

You've got this. Keep going.

CHAPTER 13

THROUGH LOVE ALL IS POSSIBLE

Love is the energy that reaches the places and spaces we believe are unreachable. It has the power to soften the hardest edges and mend what feels unbendable, and it reminds us that healing is always possible. Love doesn't demand that you be perfect. It meets you where you are—in your pain, your fear, and your doubt—and offers you a way forward. It's not loud or dramatic; most of the time, love shows up in the quietest moments, asking you to simply let it in.

Love is so much more than an emotion—it's a force. A force that transforms everything it touches. Love moves beyond the limits you place on yourself and the world around you— dissolving the barriers— that keep you from stepping fully into who you are meant to be. Love reveals our wholeness, even when we feel broken.

When we choose love—when we actively embrace it in ourselves, see it in others, and in our lives—it creates an energy that moves outward. Fear loses its grip. Pain starts to dissolve. The walls you've built out of self-protection start to crumble, and in their place, a deeper truth begins to rise.

Love is the connection that carries you from survival to significance, from resistance into alignment.

Take a moment to be honest with yourself. Where in your life are you holding love at arm's length? Is it in the way you speak to yourself, doubting your worth or holding on to shame from the past? Is it in your relationships, where fear or resentment keeps you from showing up fully? Or is it in the way you view your circumstances, resisting instead of allowing?

Now imagine, just for a moment, what could change if you let love in. Not all at once but in small, intentional ways. What if you aligned yourself with Grace instead of criticism? What if you opened your heart just a little more to someone who matters to you? What if you allowed love to flow into the parts of your life where it feels hardest to access?

This is your invitation to allow this force fully into your being. Love unlocks every door, removes every block, and brings you back to yourself in every moment. Love isn't something you have to earn—because you are made from it. Source is love. You are love.

It's already here, waiting for you to feel your connection with it. Love is in every cell, every organ, every particle of energy. Tune in.

THE LAYERS OF LOVE

Love begins within. It's the energy from which we are created, yet it is the very thing many of us struggle to offer ourselves. Self-love isn't indulgent or selfish—it's union with the divine. It's the foundation of every connection we forge, the lens through which we see the world, and the key to understanding the divine frequency of love itself.

But in this realm, self-love often feels like the most difficult love to feel. The weight of guilt, shame, and societal conditioning tells us we must earn it—that it's reserved for when we achieve, prove, or perfect ourselves. These blocks cloud the truth: that you are inherently worthy of love, simply because you exist—you are made of love.

When I reflect on my own journey, I see the decades I spent feeling disconnected from love. I sought love externally, in validation, in achievements, in others' approval. Yet, no matter how much I received, the emptiness was still there. My turning point came when I realized the love I longed for was not something I needed to seek—it was something I had to remember. Love was already within me, waiting for me to pay attention to it. When I connected to the love within me, a portal opened. The world softened. The obstacles I had once viewed as insurmountable dissolved, not because they disappeared but because I stopped standing in my own way.

Our connection with self-love is cultivated; it's a daily commitment to meet yourself with compassion instead of judgment.

Love lives in the moments where we choose the energy of Grace, even when we feel we've fallen short, in the spaces where we set boundaries to honor our energy, and when we forgive ourselves in the moments we believed we were unworthy. It's felt when we sit in silence and remind ourselves that we are enough. Love only asks for presence. And in that presence, your healing happens.

Loving others, especially those who've hurt you, challenges you to expand beyond the limits of your comfort. It's not about allowing harmful actions or dismissing your pain—because true love of those around us is an act of understanding, not access. Love will ask you to look beyond the surface and recognize the humanity—the wounds, the fears, the struggles—that may have driven their behavior.

Forgiveness through love doesn't condone the harm done, but it does free you from the chains that hurt places around your heart.

Forgiveness is a radical act of self-liberation. Holding onto resentment is like clutching a hot coal, hoping it will burn someone else. When you choose to let go, when you choose forgiveness through love, you reclaim the energy resentment once consumed.

Through love, we see that others are reflections of us. Their actions may trigger your wounds, but they also offer you an opportunity to heal. When you approach your relationships with love as your guide, you transform not only how you relate to others but also how you relate to yourself. When you expand love to a universal awareness, you begin to see the interconnectedness of all things.

Love, at its highest frequency, moves beyond the personal and into the collective. It asks us to embrace the truth that we are not separate. Every being, every experience, every fragment of existence is woven together in a web of energy.

Universal love doesn't mean bypassing pain or pretending that life is without suffering. It means holding the entirety of existence—the joy and the sorrow, the beauty and the chaos—with an open heart. It's the recognition that every challenge you face contributes to your growth, and every act of love you extend moves out into the collective.

Love, real love, is unconditional.

It doesn't waver in the face of imperfections or recoil from discomfort. Love moves mountains, heals divisions, and lifts humanity toward its highest potential. Through aligning with love, you align with Source, the energy that created us all.

> Take a moment to connect with this energy. Close your eyes and feel into the places within you that long for love's embrace. Imagine offering yourself the care you've so freely given to others. Visualize extending that same love outward, first to the people in your life and then to the world. Let it flow without condition, without limit.

You are not separate from love. You are made of it, and it's already within you, waiting for you to let it vibrate at its full capacity. When you choose to embody this energy—through self-love, love for others, and universal awareness—you align with the highest truth of who you are. And through love, all things are possible.

Love is the energy that touches the untouchable, the salve that soothes even the most invisible wounds. It operates on every level of our existence—physical, mental, emotional, and energetic—offering not just comfort but the ability to transform. Love has an innate intelligence; it knows where to flow, where to mend, and how to guide you back to yourself.

When you allow yourself to truly connect with love, you step into a state of being where healing becomes inevitable.

Love doesn't erase our pain or negate our experiences, but it transforms the meaning we assign to them. Pain becomes a portal, not a prison. Through love, you soften the sharp edges of hurt and find the strength to keep moving forward.

One of the most remarkable examples of love's healing power came from my own journey. There was a time in my life when I carried deep emotional wounds—wounds I didn't think I'd ever be able to face or heal. But in the quietest moments of surrender, love began to find a way. At first, it felt faint, almost imperceptible. A small flicker of compassion for myself. A willingness to forgive. Slowly, that flicker grew into a flame, illuminating the places I had kept in the shadows for far too long.

I worked with a woman who also had endured years of emotional trauma, carrying the weight of self-blame and unworthiness. When she began to consciously work with the energy of love—starting with herself—the transformation was undeniable. *She described it as if a fog had lifted.* The heaviness she had carried began to dissolve, not because her past changed but because love reframed her understanding of it. Through love, she realized she was not defined by what had happened to her. Instead, she reclaimed her story, finding strength and beauty in it.

Love also holds an incredible power over the physical body.

There's a reason we heal faster when surrounded by people who love us and when we practice self-compassion during difficult times. The connection between love and the nervous system is undeniable. Love brings you into a state of safety, signaling to the body that it can rest, regenerate, and heal. Love doesn't just make you feel better emotionally—it changes you on a cellular level, reminding every part of your being that you are worthy of healing.

If love heals what's broken, it also creates what's new.

Love is the energy of expansion, the force that calls forth possibility from the void. When you align with love, you align with the frequency of Source . . . your Creator. Love is what breathes life into your dreams and bridges the gap between desire and manifestation. Manifestation begins with energy. What you believe, feel, and vibrate at determines what you draw into your reality. And love? Love is the highest vibration there is. When you embody love—whether it's self-love, love for others, or universal love—you shift your energy in a way that invites abundance, joy, and alignment into your life.

I've witnessed the creative power of love in my own life time and time again. When I shifted my energy from lack to love, doors I didn't even know existed began to open. Opportunities found their way to me, relationships deepened, and life began to flow in ways that felt both effortless and miraculous. Love doesn't just bring us what we want; it brings us what we need—what our soul longs for, even if we can't articulate it.

I had a client come to me frustrated and stuck, feeling as though every effort made to move was met with resistance. Together, we explored the ways fear and doubt were blocking her from embodying love—for herself, her process, and the life she was trying to create. As she began to release those blocks and align with love, her reality shifted. Signs and synchronicities started flowing, and opportunities showed up that were better than anything she had imagined for herself. *It wasn't just coincidence—it was love in action.*

Aligning with love isn't about bypassing hard work or effort. It's about infusing that work with intention, trust, and openness. When you create from a place of love, your energy becomes magnetic to it.

Love doesn't force—it flows.

And that flow creates an energetic wave, transforming not just your life but the collective experience as a whole.

Love's creative power reminds you that you are a co-creator with the universe. Every thought, every intention, and every action carries energy. When you root yourself in love, you align with the divine, and creation becomes a partnership. You move from striving to allowing, from resistance to surrender, trusting that love will carry you exactly where you need to go. Divine timing and purpose becomes your new normal.

LOVE VS. LACK

At the heart of every decision we make lies a simple but profound choice: love or lack. These two energies shape how you experience the world, how you respond to challenges, and how you create your life. Love is expansive, abundant, and infinite. Lack, on the other hand, contracts, limits, and restricts. While love says, "There is more than enough," lack whispers, "There will never be enough."

Choosing love over lack requires awareness because lack often disguises itself as practicality, fear, or control. It tells you to settle, to play small, to guard your heart because love feels too risky. But here's the truth: Lack is an illusion, a construct of the mind that stems from fear. Love, however, is real. It is the essence of who you are, a boundless energy that connects you to Source and to one another.

When you choose love, you dismantle lack at its roots. Love expands your perception, showing you possibilities that fear and lack had hidden from view. It reminds you that you are not separate from abundance; you are a part of it. Choosing love in a moment of doubt can change everything. Instead of clinging to what feels safe, you take a leap with Faith, trusting that love will catch you. Instead of focusing on what's missing, you focus on what you can give. In doing so, you open yourself to receiving in ways you couldn't have imagined.

I've spent time feeling trapped in cycles of scarcity—financially, emotionally, and spiritually. I had to evolve through this too. Every decision I made for a period was from a place of fear, convinced there wasn't enough love and money to go around. But I began exploring what it would look like to choose love instead of lack. I started small: expressing gratitude for what I did have, offering kindness to myself in the moments of self-doubt, and opening my heart to opportunities rather than bracing for imminent failure. The shift was gradual but clearly life changing. Where I once saw barriers, I began to see openings. My relationships improved, financial opportunities floated to the surface, and, most importantly, I felt a deep sense of peace I hadn't known before.

Love is not passive; it's an active choice.

It's the decision to trust when fear tells you not to. It's the willingness to see abundance where lack wants you to focus on limitation. It's the commitment to give freely, knowing that in the flow of giving and receiving, you will always have what you need. When you choose love, you invite expansion. You step into a space where creativity flows, relationships thrive, and opportunities align. Lack, by its nature, cannot co-exist with love. Where love is present, the illusion of lack dissolves, and you are reminded of the truth: *You are whole, you are enough, and you are deeply connected to an abundant universe.*

So, ask yourself: In this moment, are you choosing love or lack? Every time you choose love, you align with your highest, most authentic self, and the universe responds in kind.

The alchemy of love is life changing. It heals what is broken and creates what is new, reminding you of your infinite potential. Love's transformative power doesn't require you to do anything other than let it in. And as you do, you begin to witness the magic it creates—not just in your life but in the world around you.

Take a moment to reflect: *Where in your life could love be a healing force? Where could love breathe life into something new?* Trust that love is always available to you. It's in your breath, your being, and your very existence.

When you allow yourself to embrace the fullness of love, you step into the truth of who you are—creator, healer, and an infinite being of light. Love is the energy that transforms, transcends, and makes all things possible.

Love, at its core, is infinite, boundless, and unconditional.

It's our energy, the frequency we're born from and meant to embody. Yet, for so many, love feels elusive—a distant possibility rather than an innate truth. Why? Because the pathway to love is often obstructed by beliefs, societal programming, and the ever-watchful ego, each weaving illusions that make love seem just out of reach. To understand how to embrace love, we must first understand what stands in its way.

One of the deepest wounds humanity carries is the belief that we are unworthy of love. This belief is so pervasive that it often goes unnoticed, silently shaping how we see ourselves and interact with the world. It whispers insidious lies: "You are not enough. You have to earn love. You are broken, flawed, unlovable." This illusion is powerful because it strikes at the heart of our existence. Love, after all, is the energy that connects us to Source, to others, and to ourselves. When we feel unworthy of love, we disconnect from this energy, building walls to shield ourselves from the very thing we crave the most. These walls, though protective in appearance, are prisons in disguise, keeping us isolated in fear and self-doubt.

The roots of unworthiness are often planted early. A harsh word from a caregiver, a rejection, or a failure becomes internalized as proof that we are undeserving. As these moments accumulate, they shape a narrative—a story you tell yourself about who you are. But here's the truth: This story is not real. It is a fabrication of the mind, a distortion born from pain.

Overcoming the illusion of unworthiness requires courage. It requires looking inward with compassion and having the courage to rewrite the narrative. It starts with small acts of love toward yourself—acknowledging your feelings without judgment, forgiving yourself for mistakes, and celebrating even the smallest victories.

I carried the weight of unworthiness like a second skin for decades. Every relationship I entered was riddled with fear—that I would be abandoned, that I wasn't enough. But by moving through the very path in this book, I uncovered the origins of this belief, tracing it back to my childhood where love was conditional. Slowly, I challenged the narrative. I wrote letters of forgiveness; practiced looking in the mirror and saying, "I love you"; and allowed myself to receive kindness from others without questioning its authenticity. Over time, the walls I built began to crumble, revealing how ready I was to embody love.

The truth is, we are all worthy of love—not because of what we do but because of who we are. Love isn't something we earn; it's something we embody.

While unworthiness often originates within, it is reinforced by the world around us.

Society, in its quest for order and structure, has conditioned us to place limits and conditions on love. We are taught that love is transactional: "If you achieve this, you will be loved. If you look like this, you will be lovable. If you conform to these standards, love will come to you." These messages are everywhere—in advertising, in social media, in the stories we consume. They paint love as something scarce and conditional, something to be earned or fought for. They pit us against one another, creating competition where there should be connection.

Cultural norms often dictate who is "deserving" of love and who is not, imposing barriers based on gender, race, sexuality, and other arbitrary markers. These barriers foster division, perpetuating the illusion that love is exclusive rather than inclusive. But love is expansive. It doesn't discriminate or withhold. Breaking free from these societal constructs requires us to question the narratives we've been handed. It requires us to see love not as a finite resource but as an infinite energy. When we stop measuring love by society's standards, we create space for love to flow freely—not just toward ourselves but toward others. We become a conduit for love.

I worked with a man who believed showing love made him weak. Society taught him that vulnerability was a flaw, that strength meant suppressing emotion. But beneath his stoic exterior was a soul longing for connection. Through our conversations, he began to challenge these cultural narratives. He allowed himself to cry, to express gratitude, and to say, "I love you," without fear of judgment. And in doing so, he found a strength far greater than he had ever known—the strength to love without conditions.

Imagine a world where we no longer let society dictate the terms of love. A world where love is given freely, without expectation or limitation. This is the world we are capable of creating when we dismantle the barriers society has imposed on us.

One of the most persistent obstacles to love is the ego.

The ego is the part of you that seeks control, and defines itself through separation and judgment. It thrives on comparison, convincing you that you are better than, worse than, or different from others. In doing so, it erects barriers to love, creating division where there could be unity.

The ego resists love because love dissolves the very foundation on which it stands. Love is unifying, boundary-less, and inclusive. It leaves no room for the ego's need to be right, superior, or in control. As a result, the ego fights back, creating stories of fear and doubt to keep love at bay.

One of the ego's favorite tools is judgment. It judges others, creating distance between you and them. It judges you, reinforcing feelings of unworthiness. It tells you that love is dangerous, that vulnerability will lead to pain, that it's safer to keep your heart closed.

But the ego is not your enemy. It is a part of you, and like all parts, it can be healed and integrated. Overcoming the ego's resistance to love requires awareness. It requires recognizing when the ego is speaking and gently redirecting your focus back to love. Meditation, mindfulness, and self-reflection are powerful tools for quieting the ego. In the stillness, you can observe its stories without becoming entangled in them. You can choose to respond with love rather than react with fear.

I guided a woman in private sessions who was completely overwhelmed with resentment toward her family. The ego had convinced her that holding on to anger was a form of protection, a way to maintain control. But in reality, it was keeping her from the love she deeply desired. Through mindfulness practices and meditation, she began to see the ego's role in perpetuating her pain. She learned to forgive—not for their sake but for her own. And in forgiving, she freed herself, creating space for love to return.

The ego will always try to protect you, but it often mistakes love for a threat.

When you understand this, you can meet the ego with compassion, reminding it that love is not something to fear. Love is safety. Love is home. And when the ego realizes this, it relaxes and reorients toward love.

The obstacles to love are real, but they are not insurmountable. Each one—whether it's the illusion of unworthiness, societal conditioning, or the ego's resistance—is a call to awaken. A call to remember who you truly are: a *being of love, deserving of love, capable of love, made of love.*

To reclaim love, we must be willing to confront these obstacles with courage and compassion. We must be willing to question the narratives we've inherited, to challenge the beliefs we've internalized, and to soften the defenses we've built.

Love is not something we need to find; it is something we need to uncover. It is already within us, waiting patiently for us to remember. And when we do, the obstacles that once seemed so large begin to dissolve, revealing a path to love that was always there.

So, ask yourself: What stands in the way of love in your life? And what would it feel like to let that obstacle go?

Love is a feeling and an action; it's a practice, a choice you make moment by moment. It's the thread that weaves meaning into your life, connecting you to yourself and to another.

While love may seem grand and unattainable at times, it's often the smallest actions—those moments of presence, kindness, and vulnerability—that hold the greatest power.

Practicing love in daily life doesn't require a monumental effort or perfect circumstances. It begins with a willingness to show up—to open your heart even when it feels easier to close it. It's about infusing love into the seemingly mundane, making it a conscious part of how you move through the world.

The first step in practicing love is recognizing that every moment holds an opportunity to embody it. Love can be as simple as offering a genuine smile to a stranger or pausing to truly listen to someone without judgment or distraction. These small actions may seem insignificant, but they carry an energy that moves outward, often in ways you cannot see.

One of the most powerful ways to practice love is through gratitude. Gratitude is the language of the heart, a way of acknowledging the beauty and abundance that already exists in your life. Start by creating a daily gratitude ritual—whether it's journaling three things you're grateful for each morning or pausing before meals to silently express thanks. Gratitude shifts your perspective, opening you to receive and give love more freely.

Active listening is another powerful expression of love. In a world that moves so fast, where distractions are constant, simply being fully present with someone is a rare and precious gift. The next time you're in conversation, set down your phone, make eye contact, and listen—not just to respond but to understand. This act of presence communicates, "I see you. You matter."

Even in challenging moments, love can find its way. For instance, when someone frustrates you, instead of reacting with anger, pause and breathe. Ask yourself, "What would love do here?" Perhaps love would choose compassion, recognizing that the person before you is also carrying unseen struggles. This doesn't mean you bypass boundaries or ignore your feelings—it means you respond with intention rather than reaction, allowing love to guide your actions. There will be times when moving from love means moving away from people, places, and spaces. Honor both.

There's a special magic in kindness given without expectation.

A random act of kindness can brighten someone's day in ways you may never know. Buy coffee for the person behind you in line. Leave an encouraging note on a co-worker's desk. Send a heartfelt text to someone who's been on your mind.

A friend of mine shared with me how she started practicing random acts of kindness after feeling disconnected in her life. Every Friday, she chose one small act—a bouquet of flowers left on a neighbor's doorstep, paying for a stranger's gas, or simply complimenting someone in the grocery store. Over time, these acts didn't just impact others; they transformed her. She began to feel more connected, more alive, and more in tune with the energy of love.

Kindness is contagious. A single act has the power to inspire others, creating a chain reaction of love. You may never see the full extent of your impact but trust that your kindness leaves a mark far greater than you realize.

Practicing love when everything is going well is easy. The real challenge—and opportunity—lies in bringing love into difficult moments.

One of the hardest places to practice love is with yourself. *When you make a mistake, when you fall short of your expectations, how do you respond?* For many, the instinct is to criticize, to shame, to withdraw. *But what if, instead, you chose love?*

One of my community members who struggled with perfectionism felt like every misstep was a failure, reinforcing her belief that she wasn't good enough. Together, we worked on shifting her inner dialogue. Instead of berating herself, she began practicing self-compassion, speaking to herself as she would a friend. "It's okay to feel disappointed. You're still learning. I'm proud of you for trying." This shift didn't happen overnight, but over time, it softened her relationship with herself, allowing love to take root where judgment once lived.

In relationships, love in action often looks like forgiveness. Holding on to resentment may feel like power, but it only keeps you chained to the past. Forgiveness doesn't mean condoning hurtful behavior; it means releasing its hold on your heart, creating space for healing.

Through 1:1 work, I guided a woman who struggled to forgive her father for years of emotional distance. Through our sessions, she came to see forgiveness not as a gift to him but as freedom for herself. She wrote him a letter—not to send but to express all the emotions she had bottled up. With each word, she felt lighter. And while their relationship didn't transform overnight, her choice to release the resentment allowed her to approach him with greater openness, paving the way for a deeper connection.

THE ENERGETIC EFFECT OF LOVE

Every act of love, no matter how small, contributes to something far greater than ourselves. When we choose love, we not only uplift those directly around us but also add to the collective energy of love in the world. Imagine you throw a pebble into a still pond. The waves move outward, touching every part of the surface, even the edges far beyond where the pebble landed. Love works the same way. A single act of love creates an energetic movement, spreading far beyond what we can see. Every act adds to a greater energy.

A community member of mine shared a story about this very effect. She was having a terrible day and decided to grab a coffee to reset. When the barista handed her the coffee, she said with a smile, "This one's on the house. You look like you could use a little extra kindness today." That small gesture completely shifted her energy. Inspired, she decided to pay it forward, offering to help an overwhelmed colleague later that afternoon. Her colleague, in turn, went home in a better mood, bringing more patience and love to her family. The barista's single act of kindness had set off a chain reaction, uplifting multiple lives.

When we choose love, we are co-creators of a better world. We may not always see the immediate results of our actions but trust that they are there, blossoming in ways that add to the greater good.

Practicing love is about showing up, even when it's hard, even when you don't feel like it. It's about trusting that love, when given freely, will always return to you in some form. *So, how will you bring love into action today? What small, intentional act can you take to infuse love into your life and the lives of those around you?* Start where you are, with what you have.

Because love, in all its simplicity and power, begins with you.

Love is limitless.

It does not rely on external conditions or favorable circumstances to thrive. True love exists beyond what is happening *to* us—it is a choice we make *within* us. This kind of love transcends emotions tied to fleeting moments of joy or connection; it's a force that remains steady, even in the face of pain, conflict, or uncertainty.

Choosing love beyond your circumstances doesn't mean ignoring reality or denying hardship. Instead, it's the practice of anchoring yourself in love, no matter how turbulent life becomes. *It's easy to love when the world feels kind and people treat you well, but what about when life feels harsh and unfair? What about when someone tests your patience or wounds your heart?* These moments are where the expansiveness of love reveals itself as more than an emotion—it becomes an energy of courage and strength.

One of my clients, who's navigating a difficult divorce, shared how she initially resisted the idea of loving her ex through the process. "Why should I offer love to someone who has hurt me so deeply?" she asked. Yet, as she began shifting her focus from anger to compassion—not for his actions but for the pain they both were carrying—she discovered a newfound freedom. Choosing love didn't change the situation, but it did transform how she moved through it. By releasing her need to hold on to resentment, she reclaimed her power, allowing love to guide her toward healing and peace in this next phase of her life.

When you choose to love beyond circumstance, you liberate yourself from being tethered to the external. This kind of love is radical because it asks you to trust that the Source of love is infinite—that it is never diminished by what you face.

Love and Faith are inseparable, connected and amplifying each other.

Faith sustains love when it feels impossible, and love gives Faith her power to transform. Together, they form an energy that has the capacity to turn challenges into opportunities, wounds into wisdom, and fear into freedom.

When you choose to love without conditions, you are tapping into a force greater than yourself. This is the essence of Faith—the energy of something unseen but profoundly felt. Faith reminds you that even when the path is unclear, love is always guiding you. She whispers, "Keep going. Trust that this moment, no matter how difficult, is part of something greater. Something for your greater good."

I had a community member who described Faith as "the tether to love." She had been caring for her father through a long illness and was exhausted by the physical and emotional toll it took. There were days when her love for him felt buried beneath resentment and fatigue. But she leaned on Faith—the feeling that her efforts were meaningful, that her love mattered, even when it felt unreturned. She began to notice glimmers: her father's eyes lighting up when she entered the room and the peace she felt after simply holding his hand. Faith transformed her experience, renewing her ability to give love freely, even when it wasn't easy.

Faith in love is not naive; the energy commits you to seeing the unseen and believing in possibilities that have yet to unfold.

It's the trust that love has the power to heal, to rebuild, and to carry you through even the darkest times.

What does it mean to embody love as a way of being? It begins with the realization that love is not something you give or receive—it's something you *are.* To live as love is to carry it in your every thought, word, and action, allowing it to shape how you see yourself, others, and the world.

Living as love doesn't mean you'll never feel anger, sadness, or frustration. These emotions are part of the human experience, and to deny them would be to deny yourself. But to embody love is to meet these emotions with compassion and Grace, choosing not to let them define you. It's the practice of asking, "How can I bring love into this moment?" and trusting that the answer will always lead you toward truth.

Living as love also requires vulnerability. It asks you to let down your walls, to open your heart fully, even when there's a risk of pain. But this is the paradox of love: The more you give, the more you receive. The more you allow yourself to be seen and known, the deeper your connection to love becomes.

One of the most beautiful aspects of living as love is the way it radiates outward. When you embody love, you create an energetic effect that touches everyone you encounter. A single smile, a kind word, or a simple gesture of care can ignite love in others, creating a chain reaction that has no end. To live as love is not always easy, but it is always worth it. It's the ultimate act of aligning with Faith, trusting that love will guide you, even when the way forward is unclear. It's the decision to let love be your compass, your anchor, and your home.

Love is not just something you do; it's who you are. When you strip away fear, judgment, and limitation, what remains is love—a limitless, all-consuming energy that connects us all.

Living as love means stepping into this truth, making love the foundation of your every choice, the essence of your being. It means trusting that love is always enough, that it is the force capable of transforming not just your life but the world around you.

So, how will you choose love today? How will you let it shape your actions, your thoughts, and your heart? Because the truth is love doesn't wait for perfect moments. It waits for you—to choose it, to embody it, to live as it.

Through love, all is possible.

FINAL THOUGHTS

Love is the most transformative force we have. It has the power to soften what feels unyielding, to mend what feels broken, and to illuminate even the darkest of paths. Love asks us to go beyond what is comfortable, to trust in its endless capacity, and to see that it is not something we seek but something we *are.*

When we choose to align with love, we align with the very energy of who we are meant to be.

Where in your life can you let love in? Is it in a relationship that has been tested or perhaps in how you see yourself? Is it in your ability to forgive, to show kindness, or to see possibility where doubt once resided? Choose an area, and invite love to take its place there. Let it soften the edges, bring clarity, and guide you forward.

No matter where you are on your journey or how far you feel you've strayed, love is always available to you. It doesn't judge how long it's been or how broken you feel—it simply waits for you to say yes. Yes to its healing. Yes to its light. Yes to its unyielding belief in your worth.

Through love, all is possible. Choose it today and every day after. You are so loved, so held, and so capable of living as the boundless force of love that you already are.

You've got this. Keep going.

ACKNOWLEDGMENTS

I think the best place for me to start in acknowledging all of the amazing souls who've helped bring this book to life is for me to say thank you to the Guides who've held my hand and shared their wisdom with me as I've pulled through all of the amazing information and guidance contained in this book. Channeling and communing with Spirit has changed me and my life for the better and I'm beyond honored to walk and share this path.

Sammantha, you saw me when I couldn't see myself. You will always be the soul who sat in the darkest depths of the crossroads and reminded me of the frequency of Grace. Thank you for knowing I could do better. Thank you for being the trusted voice beyond the veil. Thank you for walking me home to myself. I have an eternity of gratitude for you.

Jaime and Rachel, you two were sent into my life when I had to let everyone else go. I'm so grateful for the support and joy you both bring into my life. Watching you grow in your own ways is so rewarding to observe. Thank you for being my chosen family. Life would be so boring without you both.

To Ledian and Danielle, thank you for being the supportive forces that help me not only open my gifts, but master them. I'm forever appreciative for our lifetimes of connection. When I can't see the path myself, you have earned my trust. Thank you.

To my parents, Dad and Linda, thank you for giving me the space to heal and reminding me every time I feel like quitting that I've got this, if I just keep going. Linda, thank you for being the motherly love I needed. Dad, thank you for being the steady force that ensures I always have a place to call home. I love you both so much.

To my clients and community members, I appreciate you all so much. You've ebbed and flowed and grown in your own ways right along with me. Thank you for trusting me on the path of walking yourself home.

To Michelle Pilley and Amy Kiberd, thank you for reaching out, welcoming me to Hay House and helping me bring this book, and its proper title, out into the world. Working with you both has been such a wonderful experience. Thank you.

Sally Mason-Swaab, thank you for being such a kind and compassionate editor. The magic you wield is powerful. The way you gently nudged some very impactful areas of the book out of me still mystifies me. Thank you.

To everyone at Hay House who has touched and impacted this book and its journey I am so very grateful to you. You are appreciated. Thank you.

Last but surely not least I want to thank my familiars. Sprocket and Tarak, you have kept me company and reminded me to take breaks and be silly in this process. I'm thankful we walk this life as a team. I love you. Thank you.

ABOUT THE AUTHOR

Dr. Claudia Thompson is a bridge between science and spirit, guiding you through the process of awakening and transformation. With a PhD in Physical Activity, Nutrition, and Wellness and years of experience as an educator and guide, she grounds her work in evidence-based knowledge while opening the door to higher states of consciousness.

Dr. Claudia's mission is to help souls remember who they are and live in alignment with their highest truth. As a channel, quantum activator, and intuitive guide, Dr. Claudia helps those who seek guidance to access deeper levels of awareness and personal potential.

She teaches her community to release limiting beliefs, regulate their nervous system, and step fully into their authentic selves. Her work blends science, meditation, energy practices, and soul wisdom to create transformation that touches mind, body, and spirit.

Website: **drclaudiathompson.com**

We hope you enjoyed this Hay House book. If you'd like to receive our online catalog featuring additional information on Hay House books and products, or if you'd like to find out more about the Hay Foundation, please contact:

Hay House LLC, P.O. Box 5100, Carlsbad, CA 92018-5100
(760) 431-7695 or (800) 654-5126
www.hayhouse.com® • www.hayfoundation.org

Published in Australia by:
Hay House Australia Publishing Pty Ltd
18/36 Ralph St., Alexandria NSW 2015
Phone: +61 (02) 9669 4299
www.hayhouse.com.au

Published in the United Kingdom by:
Hay House UK Ltd
1st Floor, Crawford Corner,
91–93 Baker Street, London W1U 6QQ
Phone: +44 (0)20 3927 7290
www.hayhouse.co.uk

Published in India by:
Hay House Publishers (India) Pvt Ltd
Muskaan Complex, Plot No. 3,
B-2, Vasant Kunj, New Delhi 110 070
Phone: +91 11 41761620
www.hayhouse.co.in
